Watermen

Publisher's Note

Works published as part of the Maryland Paperback Bookshelf are, we like to think, books that have stood the test of time. They are classics of a kind, so we reprint them today as they appeared when first published many years ago. While some social attitudes have changed and knowledge of our surroundings has increased, we believe that the value of these books as literature, as history, and as timeless perspectives on our region remains undiminished.

Also available in the series:

The Amiable Baltimoreans by Francis F. Beirne
The Bay by Gilbert C. Klingel
Tobacco Coast by Arthur Pierce Middleton
Young Frederick Douglass by Dickson J. Preston

Watermen

Randall S. Peffer

The Johns Hopkins University Press

BALTIMORE AND LONDON

Originally published, 1979
Third printing, 1981

Maryland Paperback Bookshelf edition, 1985

The Johns Hopkins University Press
701 West 40th Street
Baltimore, Maryland 21211
The Johns Hopkins Press Ltd., London

The paper in this book is acid-free and meets the guidelines for permanence
and durability of the Committee on Production Guidelines for Book Lon-
gevity of the Council on Library Resources.

The frontispiece and the photographs on pages 94 and 124 are by M. E.
Warren; those on pages 2 and 46 are by Robert de Gast.

Library of Congress Cataloging in Publication Data

Peffer, Randall S.
  Watermen.

  1. Oyster fisheries—Maryland—Tilghman Island. 2. Oyster fisheries—
Chesapeake Bay. 3. Fishermen—Maryland—Tilghman Island. 4. Tilghman
Island, Md. I. Title.
  SH365.M3P43   974.2'32   79-9896
  ISBN 0-8018-2177-0 (hardcover)
  ISBN 0-8018-2737-X (paperback)

To Marilyn and Noah
who follow the water

One day after we'd caught our limit of oysters we were all up to the Carpenter Street Tavern (in St. Michaels), and Randy told us he had written a book about the watermen. He wanted our opinion about whether he had told about us right, so he read about a time when Billy and Ginny Adams had a showdown with the Marine Police. It was comic: Randy reading kind of shy and quiet and Miss Ginny breaking in every few seconds like she was in church with "that's right, tell it like it is!" What it did was make us laugh. Then Randy said he was going to change everyone's name to protect our privacy. I thought Ginny was going to have a hemorrhage the way she stood up to Randy and said, "Don't you dare change my name. I want it in that book. You told the truth about everything and I want you to tell the truth about my name!" Ginny wasn't fooling around. I believe we all agreed with her. We're proud to be watermen. I told Randy to go right ahead and use my name. The rest did the same.

Bart Murphy
Captain of the *Ruby G. Ford*

Open Season

n the first Saturday of November the skipjacks of Tilghman Island were dressed for a ritual. The ritual was the Chesapeake Bay Appreciation Day skipjack race, which marked the beginning of the oystering season. This was to be my first season dredging oysters aboard a skipjack. The race represented a special challenge to me. It signified what workboat races always have to unseasoned sailors; it was the time to prove oneself, a rite of passage.

I had come to Bay Hundred Peninsula on Maryland's Eastern Shore from Pennsylvania's mountains where I had grown up. For several years I had been teaching English at the Mercersburg Academy, an independent school on the Mason-Dixon line. In my free time I had explored the Chesapeake Bay on the sailboats of friends, but my interest in the Bay ran deeper than sailing. According to family tradition my colonial ancestors had settled the Eastern Shore in the seventeenth century. They were called "watermen" and they made their living harvesting the Chesapeake's oysters, crabs, fish, and waterfowl.

Watermen still dominate life on the Eastern Shore, and I began investigating their communities. Tilghman Island fascinated me because of its remoteness and its wharves lined with working sailboats. The island sits just off the southern end of Bay Hundred Peninsula and marks the northern entrance to the Chesapeake's largest river, the Choptank. Tilghman is a twenty-mile sail southeast across the Bay from Annapolis, and a twenty-two–mile highway journey from the "capital" of the Eastern Shore, Easton, Maryland. The island measures more than three and a half miles from north to south and less than a mile east to west. Farms and scattered houses spread over the southern half of the island to Black Walnut Point. A community of modest frame homes stretches to the northern shore of Tilghman where Knapps

Narrows, a 150-foot broad channel of swift current, cuts islanders off from Bay Hundred and offers dockage to most of the Chesapeake's remaining skipjack fleet. The population has remained approximately 1500 since the turn of the century. Its link to the mainland is a drawbridge across the Narrows. Most of the men work on the water.

On the morning of the race I was the first to arrive at the wharves. Images from *Captains Courageous* and *Moby Dick* flashed through my mind. I began to romanticize the lives of Tilghman Island's sailors. Then, like so many young men before me, I turned away from shore and began to chase dreams across the water. In the moonlight the hard work, worries, and hazards of dredging oysters under sail lay hidden beneath the silence of the skipjacks' dredge-winding machines, the gleam of fresh varnish on bowsprits, and the smell of new manila lines and halyards. The skipjacks, called "drudge boats," had been "corked"; the hulls sported glossy coats of white paint; the decks had been re-covered with three-quarter–inch native pine tacked with roofing nails over the leaky deck timbers; blown-out sails had been restitched and washed for "one more season"; and trailboards under the bowsprits had been rehighlighted in red, blue, and white. Most of these boats were over seventy years old, and they owed their survival to a one-hundred-year-old Maryland law that permits dredging for oysters only with a sailboat that displaces fewer than ten tons of water. The Chesapeake watermen developed the skipjack in the latter half of the nineteenth century to meet Maryland's laws. About thirty of these work boats endure and the seventeen present for the race looked fit, as though they could teach me a lesson before the day was over.

The wharves began to creak with people: not the usual crews in boots and oilskins, but women and children in slacks and sweaters, men in gold hats and sport shirts. They talked fast and laughed as a continuous stream of ice chests, beer cases, grocery bags, and cameras flowed onto the skipjacks. I heard bits of conversation.

"Honey, we get over to Annapolis this time about once either year."

"Been goin' up there ten years now."

"This here's a dumb old boat and she ain't finished the race only once. . . . Wouldn't be right to miss it though."

"Stanley Larrimore gonna win again."

"Some of these boats is smart, know what I mean?"

"No sense goin' drudgin'—ain't cold enough."

"Bunch of these fellows ain't never been drudgin' before."

"Lordy, they'll learn."

"Goin' racin'."

"Yes, sir."

One by one the Tilghman Island skipjacks cinched their push boats up against the sailboat sterns and made their way up the Bay toward the race course around Sandy Point Light (just north of Annapolis and the Chesapeake Bay Bridge). On the *Ruby G. Ford*, a forty-five-foot skipjack, the captain was Bart Murphy, a dark, thin man of forty. His vessel had been built in 1891 in Fairmont, Maryland. She registered nine gross tons, and under the captaincies of five different men from several Chesapeake ports, she had dredged oysters without a serious accident for eighty-six winters. Before her present captain gave any commands he squinted silently ahead at the water, as if wrestling with alternatives. As Bart steered the *Ruby Ford* past Poplar Island his commands came forward. They always began "Bobby" then "Haul her up," "Shake out a tuck," "Sheet out that jib."

Bobby was *Ruby Ford*'s first mate. He was a husky twenty-five-year-old with a puckish grin. Bobby found humor in grabbing crew members in headlocks with every five-degree shift in the wind. I tried to stay clear of him.

My other three crew mates were middle-aged veteran dredgers. They huddled around their captain and called me "Boy."

When the offer came to toast the sunrise with a fried egg sandwich and a beer, I grabbed at the chance. It might calm the nervousness I felt. It didn't. I paced the length of the *Ruby Ford* without trying to show concern that none of the crew was quite sure where the race began this year. I felt eyes follow me up and down the deck—Bobby.

Sails hung tall, but as Bart said, "There weren't but a breath o' wind." *Ruby Ford* glided up the Bay. The push boat's Cadillac V-8 plugged her along from astern. It was a three-hour trip north to the Bay Bridge, and Bart let everyone but me take a turn at the wheel. The crew talked about everything but the race and alternately drank beer and coffee. They clustered on the stern of the boat. To pass the time and bleed off some of the anxiety, I sat alone on the foredeck and studied the race course chart. By the time the boat reached the bridge, I could just about distinguish the navigational aids from the race course marks on the chart.

But the marks on the race chart weren't in the same places as the buoys were in the water. Was the start to the east or west of the black and white buoy, or was it over to the right there, 200 yards by that buoy six? I asked the captain. Bart squinted at the horizon—not the buoys—for a moment, then spoke, "It don't matter, we'll just follow them other boats."

The other boats came. By 10:30 A.M. seventeen working skipjacks had gathered off the beach at Sandy Point. The Bay rippled with a light southwest breeze, and Bart sent Bobby into the push boat to shut off the Cadillac. The skipper paid out the main sheet, motioned for me to take the wheel, and let *Ruby Ford* sail with the wind abeam. I turned the wheel tentatively to starboard what seemed two or three full turns, but the skipjack held her heading and drifted in the current with 1200 square feet of sails fluttering overhead.

"Honey, come over," Bart's right arm waved to starboard.

Slowly his message sunk in: "Turn the wheel, stupid." I did.

"She ain't no yacht," the captain said.

Ruby Ford was about as responsive as a tractor trailer, but after she had put me through this embarrassing pause, reminded me that I was green crew, she nosed off the wind and let the breeze fill the mainsail.

Once the skipjack gained speed, the captain told me to head toward a pair of dredge boats that had come from up the Bay. From amidship Bart called the other two skippers. "Howdy, Jesse, howdy, Christy. You boys drudge a lick this morning? Any arsters up north this year?"

"Found a rank patch, but arsters look thinner than either year, yet," came the answer.

Bart ran his hands through his thinning hair and nodded knowingly, "Lot of worry in this business; ain't gonna drudge next year if I can help it." He retrimmed the jib and gave a soft kick for luck to the horseshoe tacked on the heel of the bowsprit.

Bart Murphy hollered to bring her about. This time I spun the wheel fast and hard. *Ruby Ford* swung through the eye of the wind and trimmed up on the new point of sail. Bart saw that she did and seemed to lose interest in me and the boat.

The captain joined the other men who popped beers, fixed cheese sandwiches, and sunbathed on the work deck. I understood that I was on my own. I felt like a student pilot on his first solo—awed, anxious, exhilarated.

For the next half hour I tacked the boat at will, back and forth past a large state-owned power vessel flying a committee boat flag. Practice.

A police runabout came alongside and announced that the race was starting in ten minutes. *Ruby Ford* was heading away from the starting line, so Bart asked the police boat to push the stern around to get the boat going in the right direction. For a minute the crew came alive and joined together to haul the push boat up on the davits; then they went back to their food, beer, sun, and talk of "good lookin' women." All except Bobby, who kept circling aft around the cabin house eyeing me. We both wanted the skipper to take the helm.

I asked the captain what to do. Bart shrugged, "Don't let them other boats steal your air."

We were on a collision course with another skipjack. She was the starboard boat, and I responded according to the rules of the road committed to memory during years of pleasure sailing: I began to give way. Suddenly Bart was on his feet. "What the . . . Hold your course! That fellow's gonna chicken out."

The other fellow didn't. Both skipjack crews came to the rails and spent the next several minutes fending off, exchanging beers, casting smiles at me standing stiffly at *Ruby Ford*'s wheel, laughing and complaining about the light breezes.

"Seems like either year now we come up here and it's slick ca'm."

"Lordy-go-to-hell, ain't it so?"

The two-minute gun had gone off and here we were spooning mainsails and drifting downwind from the starting line.

Bart Murphy finally kicked *Ruby Ford* free of the "gam" and said maybe I better head the boat up toward the starting line. We weren't in bad position—still on the windward side of the fleet—but *Ruby Ford* wasn't heading upwind so well. There wasn't much time, so I suggested that the boat might sail better if the crew put down their beers long enough to trim in the sails.

The captain shook his head: "That don't do nothin' on these here boats. Pull them sails in and she won't go at all. Bobby, drop that jib." The jib came down, and *Ruby Ford* nodded closer to the wind.

The gun was about to go off, and if the breeze held, *Ruby Ford* would slosh across the line as the windward boat on a good course for the first mark, Sandy Point Light. For the first time that day I began to feel some confidence. Then fifty yards from the line, the wind died.

As the starting gun sounded I heard a clatter of engines that sounded like a pack of stock cars droning up behind *Ruby Ford*. In the next second two skipjacks brushed past our boat. They cruised over the starting line propelled by their push boats. Once over the line, they hauled the little boats aboard. They had a hundred-yard advantage on everyone else.

I cursed: "Goddamn."

Bart Murphy laughed. "Them boys want to win. Might do it, too. It don't matter—hold your course—on Monday we'll catch just as many arsters as them boats. Relax."

I sat back on the steering box and held the course. The crew came aft and sat around on the cabin house and atop the davits. Bobby handed me a sandwich and a beer. The guys talked about the good summer crabbing, log canoe racing, hunting this fall, and where the crew might go in Florida for a vacation in the spring. On other dredge boats people lounged around as they did on *Ruby Ford*. Young men mingled with old men. I began to see that the goals for this race day grew as light as the breeze: cross the starting line, stay close to the other dredge boats, and do what you can to fix this warm carefree day of sailing in your mind. Race day was not for worrying; those days lay ahead.

Ruby Ford sailed herself, and the crew seized the day. For four hours we drank, joked, and drifted the distance to Sandy Point Light. I was called by my first name. Gradually the current set *Ruby Ford* parading through a spectator fleet of several hundred yachts. The pleasure sailors toasted us and clicked cameras. We obliged. Bobby and I found reasons to monkey out on the bowsprit. Bart and the others found poses that gave just the right flavor of casual ruggedness to the comments they directed at the gapers in the spectator fleet: "Don't let your son go drudgin'," "Man's crazy to follow the water." "She's just a dumb old boat, eighty-six years this season, but she'll still catch a lick o' arsters."

The watermen enjoyed being a spectacle, but they were beginning to cultivate a more serious attitude toward the winter ahead. Food and beer were running low, and the sun ducked behind a thick bank of clouds. The wind kicked up and the air grew cold. It smelled like a winter squall brewing. Stanley Larrimore was way out in front. No doubt he was going to win the race as the voices on the wharf had said. He always did. But it didn't matter to any of the *Ruby Ford*'s crew. They had other things on their minds: the weather and oysters. We turned tail and ran for Tilghman Island.

South of Love Point Bart Murphy started up the winding machine. He spent twenty minutes tinkering with the carburetor, then ordered us to heave over the oyster dredges. Bobby and I worked together. *Ruby Ford* shuddered as the dredges raked over an oyster bar. When we hauled the dredges in, emptied them, and culled the catch, we had more than three bushels of keepers from one lick.

"It's a fair catch here, is what it is . . . if the wind lays to west'ard," mumbled Murphy to himself. He threw a Clorox bottle overboard to mark the spot. It was tethered by twenty-five feet of line to a length of pipe. The wind blew out of the west. I knew where I would be Monday morning.

Oyster season opened. On a sunless morning twenty skipjacks nodded their bowsprits over the currents of Knapps Narrows and the shadows of Dogwood Cove. The oyster sloops groaned in gusts of snow. Halyards slapped rapidly on the masts. The wind blew out of the west at twenty knots. Even if the snow kept up, I knew we would leave port: this was the weather Tilghman Islanders called a "drudger's breeze."

Ruby Ford pitched among the pack of similar dredge boats. Although she was the oldest skipjack in the fleet, she lacked none of the grace of the younger boats (most of which were built between 1900 and 1925). Her long clipper bow, raked mast, low-slung white hull, and push boat swaying astern on davits disguised the *Ruby G. Ford*'s broad fifteen-foot deck. Like a barge her flat bottom drew only three and a half feet of water with the centerboard up. Yet *Ruby Ford* had the character of a tall ship: mast hoops, leg-o'-mutton rig, manila lines, cotton jib, spiderweb-like lazyjack lines on the club jib and main boom, enough wooden blocks to make an antique dealer drool, and a Richardson steering wheel dated 1889.

After less than a week's work, *Ruby Ford* looked worn to me. Not only was her paint chipped and rust-streaked from weather and work, but her deck looked like a junkyard. The large gasoline engine and winding machine gears amidship were the guts of the dredging operation. Six man-sized iron and net cages that were the oyster dredges leaned against the mast, the winding machine housing, and each other. That was just the beginning. Shovels, open oil drums, buckets, sawhorses, air-cooled bilge pumps, propane gas containers, boxes full of rusty fittings, tools, tarps, oilskins, and what seemed dozens of rubber gloves were scattered over the boat. Everything was streaked with gray mud and bits of oyster shells.

I walked up and down the wharf to keep warm. After several minutes I heard a pickup truck bang up the road over frozen ruts and lurch to a stop. Three men jumped out of the back and two more piled from the cab—*Ruby Ford*'s crew. They shuffled along the wharf awkwardly in thermal underwear, jeans, layers of sweaters, parkas, and hip boots. Crews stirred on other boats. They complained. Their skipjacks were from "down Bay," and they lived aboard in the forecastles while their boats were working the rich oyster beds off Tilghman Island. From the complaints voiced by some of the down-Bay watermen, it seemed that *Ruby Ford*'s crew wasn't missing much of the romance by living at home.

We boarded the vessel. No one spoke. The cook went below deck and sent a yellow light shining from the cabin companionway across the steering wheel of the *Ruby Ford*. Bart Murphy busied himself priming a gasoline bilge pump. Bobby and I opened the hatch over the oyster hold and checked the water level in the bilges. *Ruby Ford* had taken on eight inches of water during the night. We lowered the siphon hose into the bilge. The captain started the pump.

Bobby and I joined the cook and the rest of crew. In *Ruby Ford*'s cabin the watermen seemed jammed into a boat a quarter of a skipjack's size. There was no passageway leading through the forward bulkhead. What made my claustrophobia worse was the way the bulkhead was lined with shelving containing more coffee making materials than a diner. A propane gas stove hissed almost in center cabin, and the six of us huddled together in the eight-by-eight room. There was not quite standing headroom. I sat on a quarter berth (a fourteen-inch plank). Behind it I could see spare parts stashed in the bilges: plank and spare timber, life jackets, old lines, discarded pots and pans, lots of undiscernible pieces of metal, and oilskins and rubber gloves. *Ruby Ford* stank—kerosene, coffee, bacon, eggs, toast, grits, and humanity. The crew drank coffee and ate. They joked and sniped at each other. Two young whites and two older blacks traded racial jests. I tried to laugh at the appropriate times.

Where was the captain? Off trying to decide where to go "drudgin'." The crew tried to second-guess their captain, but after much speculation as to where the *Ruby Ford* would work today they admitted that they did this every morning and were always wrong. One of the men cursed the early hour. Another cursed the weather. Then the Bay. Then the crew. Then the boat. The cursing stopped. The watermen seemed to know they had gone too far; they changed the subject.

Bobby teased the black cook; "You marry that old lady of yours yet, Bernard?"

"Shit, no. I too smart and too young for that. I seen what marriage do for you. Get your white ass in one goddamn sling . . ."

A pair of boots attached to a muddy blue insulated suit dropped through the companionway—Bart Murphy. The jibes ceased and the question was asked, "Where we drudgin' today?"

"River," said Murphy in a way that made it plain that he resented being questioned by crew.

The smiles disappeared from the crew's faces, and the conversation turned more serious. This was a matter of money. The captain wouldn't go out in the Bay because it was too rough for dredging. Today they would work the oyster bed on the eastern side of Tilghman Island in the mouth of the

Choptank River where the water was "ca'm." The oysters from the river would bring only about three dollars a bushel. Oysters from the Bay might earn six dollars.

The crew talked about the economics of the boat. During the winter season the skipjacks try to work Monday through Friday if their buyers have a market, and if the weather permits. Each workday the boat's earnings are divided into shares. One-third of the total covers the boat's needs for food, fuel, sails, rigging, planking, engines, paint, and haulout —a figure that often exceeds $10,000 a year. The remaining profits are divided equally among the captain and the five crewmen. When the boat catches its limit of 150 bushels of six-dollar oysters, a man can make $100 a day, but the average earnings are far below that. Skipjack crewmen might make $5,000 in a season. All of them "go crabbin'" during the summer. They didn't much need days like this.

Bart Murphy finished his coffee and we followed him on deck to get the *Ruby Ford* underway. A three-knot current rushed past the wharf where she tied up in Knapps Narrows. *Ruby Ford* needed to turn 180 degrees, bow into the current, in order to head east to the oysterbeds. We paid out line to lower the push boat. Then we harnessed its nose into a notch on the starboard side of the skipjack's stern. Bobby swung into the push boat and idled its V-8. The crew tried to let the current swing *Ruby Ford*'s stern around, but the bowsprit snagged on the skipjack moored inboard. For twenty minutes we pushed, pulled, and swore at the bowsprit until we sprang free of the *Seagull*.

The push boat drove *Ruby Ford* under the drawbridge that connects Tilghman Island with Bay Hundred Peninsula. We found open water. The sun hadn't come up yet, and my rubber gloves were damp from line handling. They began to freeze. It continued to snow.

We kept warm by breaking out the mud dredges (different kinds of dredges for different bottoms) and rigging them to steel cables on the winding machine. At the captain's command everyone grabbed the main halyard and heaved 1200 square feet of new dacron (the first synthetic sail the *Ruby Ford* has ever had) aloft, leaving four reefs tucked in the sail. There was no winch to stretch out the halyard— snub it, cleat it.

Astern sixteen other skipjacks worked their way out into three-foot seas. We shut down the push boat and hauled it aboard. I waited for the moment of screeching gulls, splattering waves across the bow, the snapping dacron, and the command that would bring them all to the sheets to trim sail. It never came.

Ruby Ford nodded off the wind and trimmed up untended on a beam reach. The source of this surprise: Bart Murphy had knotted the main sheet to the traveler in such a way that it appeared that this point of sail had been trimmed into the *Ruby Ford* for the season.

The dredgeboat slopped through the snow flurries at about three knots. She could take more sail. Bart Murphy felt it and called forward to pull up the shortened jib. The head sail trimmed stiff without anyone's touching a sheet.

Bart pushed a switch and the winder engine, a six-cylinder Chevy, began to cough and bang. The captain yelled "heave" and the crew chorused "ho" as we slipped the two dredges over the sides. The dredge cable creaked over the rollers amidship until the dredges began raking over the bottom.

It had been this way since 1865. That year Maryland lifted a prohibition on dredging, which had been outlawed since 1820 because it threatened to rake the upper Chesapeake clean of oysters. Lifting the ban on dredging was the Maryland legislature's reaction to political pressure from oystermen who could only harvest oysters through the slow, laborious method of plucking them from the bottom with tongs.

15

They complained that the ban placed them in a weak position to compete in the marketplace with Virginia watermen who were permitted to dredge the lower Chesapeake. Even though Maryland's new dredging law attempted to regulate the oyster harvest through limiting dredging to sailboats working on designated bars, the efficient combination of dredge and skipjack increased the Chesapeake's annual yield of oysters in the years from 1865 to 1885 from 1,000,000 to 15,000,000 bushels. After 1885 the harvest shrunk dramatically due to overfishing with the efficient dredge. However, the skipjack and dredge were here to stay. Cull law and daily limits have to save the Chesapeake oyster from extinction. In the 1977–78 season Maryland oystermen harvested 2,290,802 bushels, an average catch by the standards of the last twenty years.

As I waited for *Ruby Ford*'s dredges to fill with oysters, three skipjacks dragged dangerously close across our vessel's bow. No one seemed to notice. We were called to work by the captain speeding up the winder engine. This was his signal to us to engage the winder clutches and reel aboard the oyster dredges.

The dredge frames banged up over the rails. Two men worked each dredge. We swung the pocket-like net bag up over the side and emptied fifty pounds of muddy shells on the work deck just aft of the mast. Bart Murphy brought *Ruby Ford* about and hollered forward "heave." We sang "ho" and let the dredges slide the three fathoms back to the bottom.

Ruby Ford needed all her crew: two or three men bent spread-legged over each pile of dredgings. We culled good oysters from the piles and scooped them between our legs like dogs digging holes. Some crabs crawled among the debris. We tossed them into a spare dredge for safe-keeping (dinner). The rest of the first dredging—probably 70 percent of what we had pulled up—was refuse (old oyster shells, bottles, and beer cans). We shoveled it over the side. Someone said it was going to be "a long mother of a day." Heave, ho.

Ice built up on deck. There were no life lines, and I began to worry about working the dredge on the leeward side of the boat. It would be easy to fall overboard. Bobby and Bernard kneeled beside me culling oysters. Waves rushed regularly over the bulwark and around our legs. Each wave left more ice.

Bernard swore: "Fuck this shit. Goddamn captain goin' to drown me."

"You're just a chickenshit nigger, it's all you are, Bernard," said Bobby. "Ain't this little bit o' water, or Bart, goin' to hurt you either bit."

"What you know. You jus' too goddamn dumb to worry. I drudged for arsters 'fore you was born, and I seen all the dead niggers that washed up on this friggin' shore come drudgin' season. Some o' them old captains throw'd niggers overboard for fun. This ain't goddamn bath water, you know."

"Chickenshit. What in God's good name am I doin' workin' with this yellow-ass nigger?" Bobby shook his head in disbelief.

"Goddamn, boy. I'm tellin' you it's only the fool ain't scared o' this Bay. I seen a man get overboard in this weather. Workin' the lee drudge just like this. We's haulin' the drudge and its ice. Wham. He slips. The drudge has thrown that man overboard. In a second we throws two life rings to him, but he don't even swim for 'em—and he could swim—he just drown. Never found the body. This the worst fuckin' work. You think they call it "drudgin'" cause it's so much fun? Fuck this shit . . ."

The routine continued. By 9:30 the snow had stopped. Yet

more than twelve skipjacks hauled dredges and ran for home. The chill factor was below zero. Bobby said the other crews were chickenshits. Only two other boats continued to work. Bart Murphy paced the deck in front of the steering wheel, kicking the cabin side and hugging his shoulders to keep warm. He figured he owed the crew a conference; we had only caught about fifteen bushels of oysters.

Ruby Ford held her footing while Bart came forward from his perch at the wheel and met the crew on the working deck. Go in?

"Hell, no," said several voices. "Let's see how it goes."

"We out here, now," said Bernard. "May as well work."

The men's decision was surprising to me. For an hour I had been daydreaming about my warm rented house on Tilghman's harbor. The crew seemed too independent to want to freeze their butts off for so few oysters. But the jibes the crew had taken at the captain as they worked were misleading; they had made him seem someone to be endured like Ahab. The complaints masked respect and affection. They said Bart had a plan, and they were with him.

The crew of the *Ruby Ford* hauled dredges, shook out two reefs, and sailed three miles to different oyster beds. The first haul produced oysters the size of grapefruit. Not high quality, but a good number of "keepers." The clouds had blown away, and we were left with a bright crisp day that almost made me forget how cold it was. Bart Murphy tossed his Clorox bottle buoy overboard. Bernard brewed coffee and the crew toasted a better day.

The *Ruby Ford* dredged into the afternoon that way— sailing and resailing half-mile tacks past the Clorox bottle. Haul, heave, cull, shovel; haul, heave, cull, shovel. Thirty, fifty, eighty bushels of oysters and talk to pass the time.

The crew told stories about Vietnamese girls, guns, and boats and Eastern Shore girls, guns, and boats.

"See that old drudge boat layin' over in them shallows," said Bernard pointing to a wreck near Tilghman Island. "She had one right smart captain, you know. Boat was old and small—not much to speak of. Wouldn't catch her limit. So I guess her captain got tired o' bein' poor. 'Fuck it,' he say, and when no one is lookin' he runs the old tub ashore and fixes an illegal propeller in her. Smart? I'm tellin' you. He rigged that propeller to run off the goddamn winder motor.

"Well pretty soon that old boat begins catchin' her limit every day. She's makin' money even when there weren't hardly no sailin' breeze. 'Course she running on the propeller. The sails is just up for decoration. But the captain he ain't lettin' on cause he knows some son of a bitch might get jealous, pissed off, and shoot him. Crew? Them niggers ain't sayin' nothin' 'bout the propeller 'cause they all gettin' rich.

"But that bunch of fools gets too greedy. They be racin' that drudge boat along at ten knots every time they think no one's goin' to see 'em. Now, you know the Marine Police is dumb, but you can only fuck 'em so long in the same way before it dawns on to 'em that they's gettin' screwed. So, in this case, it dawns on to 'em and they set up a sting.

"Here's how folks tell it. The drudgers out workin' the river. It's slick ca'm. The sails is just kinda hangin' loose from the mast and that propeller just movin' the boat real pretty. And they got on some arsters, too. Them niggers is singin' cause they makin' so much money. The police, they hidin' in the cove watchin' all this through binoculars. Hell, I think they might even been takin' pictures of this boat power drudgin'.

"When the police got this all documented, they came out of the cove with the lights flashin' and the siren wailin' on their old cruiser. Well, when the drudger sees this he knowed he's in trouble. So he says the hell with it and cranks up that propeller fast as she'll go. Heads right across the flats where the cruiser can't. Runs that skipjack right up close to shore till she sticks in the mud right where she's laying now. Then the captain and the niggers wade ashore. They is long gone from Tilghman Island 'fore the police ever get back to harbor.

"That old drudge boat weren't worth much anyway. But the Department of Natural Resources revoked her license, so she ain't no good to nobody. So there she sits—one fast boat . . . for a while."

"That never happens now," said Bobby. "Somebody try to save an old wreck like that and make it a pleasure boat. I ain't shittin' ya. These yachtsmen are crazy bastards."

What followed was a commentary by Bobby on the foolishness of yachtsmen. He told how Buck Garvin, the buyer for *Ruby Ford*'s catch, got calls every week asking if he knew where there was an old dredge boat someone could make into a yacht. Bobby laughed at the idea. He knew how uncomfortable it is to live on a skipjack, and he knew that any dredge boat a waterman wants to sell must not have a solid timber in her. But according to Bobby the yachtsmen don't seem to mind: he knew of one dredge boat a pleasure sailor bought without a marine survey—that didn't matter, but the man wouldn't hand over a nickel to the former skipper until he received a written history of the boat. The antique business is good on the Eastern Shore said Bobby.

Now, finding a dredge boat to work was difficult. Bart Murphy salvaged the *Ruby G. Ford* in 1972 after she had slipped a mooring, sunk two tonging boats, lost her push boat and bowsprit, and snagged on a bar in the Choptank River. Bart had sold his first skipjack and tried tonging for oysters. But he didn't like it, and he was looking for a way to get back into dredging. By rescuing the *Ruby Ford* he avoided months of searching and haggling with other watermen who might want to give up their skipjacks. Bart was so excited the day he finished repairing *Ruby Ford* that he didn't wait to find a crew—he took his new boat dredging and caught fourteen bushels of oysters single-handedly.

The mounds of oysters rested fore and aft on both sides of the boat. If *Ruby Ford* had her 150-bushel limit the mounds would be as large as the plywood sheets braced against the rails to prevent the oysters from falling overboard. The piles weren't that big. Bernard went below to make coffee. The rest of us sought out fresh sets of rubber gloves, warmed in the boat's oven. We were the last crew out by two hours. Now it was four o'clock and time to get home while there was light.

With sails furled the *Ruby G. Ford* tied along the buyer's wharf, and a crane with a steel bushel-bucket unloaded and tallied the catch. One hundred seven bushels. Bart Murphy went to collect the money.

We rinsed down the deck and hauled the push boat aboard. I listened to Bart and Bobby talk about crashing the bars in St. Michaels—"Honey, don't it seem time they let us back in there?"

The wind died, and the sun felt warm on my cheeks. Someone joked, "Wonder if tongin's this easy?"

"Believe 'tis," said Bobby, "but social life ain't nothin'."

Bart and Bobby laughed a bit more politely when they swore themselves to good behavior if the barkeeper at St. Michaels's Carpenter Street Tavern would accept their apologies for previous indiscretions and serve up some beer. We drank Michelob. Bobby and some other dredgers dived into a discussion of an oyster tonger's lack of social life.

"Believe a tonger's like an arster: gets his kicks from changing sex in midlife," said Bobby. He looked around to see if any of the tongers at the bar wanted to take up his challenge.

At the far end of the bar sat a man and woman. The man was, in Eastern Shore parlance, raw-boned and tall. His grey work clothes, tossle cap, thinning hair, and brown face betrayed his forty-five years on the water. He smiled at the young men down the bar, "Guess you better give them drudgers some beers on me, Jake; there's too many to fight."

Ruby Ford's crew was in the process of saying "Thank ya, Cap'" to their beneficiary when the woman next to him rose from her stool and walked over to the dredgers. She was small, but in her layers of sweatshirts and jeans she looked husky. The oyster mud speckled on her face showed there wasn't much she couldn't do.

She spoke: "Let me tell you fellas something. Billy Adams, who just bought you beer, won't go drudgin' 'cause he can make a better living tonging. Billy'll get forty bushels right out here in Broad Creek. Ain't neither of you man enough to catch that many arsters by yourself."

Billy called from his stool: "C'mon, Gin, Old Black Bart's pirates is just having fun, and they know I been tonging twenty-five years 'fore my social life improved. But it didn't have to do with changing sex."

"It had to do with Gin going with you," injected the bartender. Ginny and Billy smiled.

"Believe it did," said Billy.

"Only way to be married to a waterman," said Virginia Adams.

"Only way to keep track o' him," teased a dredger.

"You know it, honey. Neither stray woman going to run a married man when his wife works on the water with him."

"Ain't like that, Ginny," said another dredger.

"How do you know? You're still raising peach fuzz."

"Been married ten years, now . . . mostly."

"Mostly! I hear you, worthless waterman. Maybe your wife's been *mostly* married, too. I could tell you where she's been seen, and it weren't dredgin'."

The dredgers bought beers all around the bar.

For me, meeting Billy and Virginia Adams was not just an evening's entertainment. It was my introduction to another element of my ancestry, the people who harvest oysters by taking them from the Bay with hand-held tongs. I was impressed by tales I had heard from the dredgers that confirmed Ginny Adams's claims of Billy's prowess—more than forty bushels a day! Ginny said she couldn't cull oysters fast enough to keep up with how quickly Billy scooped them onto their boat; if I wanted to buy a tonging license for twenty-five dollars I might go along tonging with the Adamses on days when I wasn't dredging. I was intrigued by Billy and Ginny's partnership. There were a lot of days when the wind blew too much, or too little, for the *Ruby Ford* to leave port.

It didn't blow one Thursday and Bart Murphy sent us home by 7:00 A.M.—"Ain't no use to even raise a sail in this ca'm." I drove to the Adamses' house in St. Michaels with my new tonging license. I waited half an hour before the lights came on, and it was not until after eight that Ginny, Billy, and I reached the Adamses' thirty-five-foot bay-built skiff, *Yankie*. Dredging had made me used to leaving home at 5:30 each morning on an empty stomach; the Adamses' waking with the sun and their leisurely breakfast at home spoke of luxury.

The sun was high in the sky when Billy fired up *Yankie* and drove her down Broad Creek toward a favorite oyster bar. Thick pine and walnut forests on both shores protected the boat from any high winds that might develop during the day. The tonger stood near the stern and maneuvered his boat by twisting a "joy stick" rigged by cables to the rudder.

Ginny and I stood in *Yankie*'s small cabin in the bow, smoking cigarettes and warming ourselves over a gas heater. Ginny tuned a CB radio to channel 17, a waterman's frequency, while I marveled over the extraordinary convenience of a marine head built into *Yankie*.

The radio crackled.

"This the *Casey O* callin' the *John D*, where ya at?"

"Believe I'm still in the barroom."

"Ain't either one of us made it home last night."

"We slept on the boat. Nearly froze."

"Don't you know it? Like old times. 'Fraid this cold weather's here to stay."

"Looks like it. Best make your money 'fore Christmas. Could be nothing but ice skating after that."

Ginny Adams turned down the radio and lit another cigarette. "Damn," she said. "Hope those boys are wrong 'bout the weather. No ice sheathing on this boat."

Billy heard Ginny's exclamation over the grumble of the engine and responded: "Twelve hundred dollars to put metal sheathing on this boat. I can't afford it. Just have to take my chances. Pray the ice don't get thick enough to put us out of business."

Billy held his hands over the engine's exhaust stacks for warmth: "Twenty degrees and skim ice in the middle of December. Damn, if it don't look like hard times down the road."

"Don't think about it, Billy," said Ginny. "I can always go back to work at the ribbon factory. We won't starve."

"Hardly." Billy cut *Yankie*'s engine, slipped up to the bow, and threw overboard a heavy bar of metal, scavenged from an abandoned railroad track. The metal was tied to dacron rope: this was a drag anchor for holding *Yankie* semistationary over the oyster bar.

Billy Adams moved quickly—peeling out of his heavy coat, selecting a set of tongs with eighteen-inch shafts from the five pairs spanning the length of *Yankie*'s work deck, and dipping his tongs down to the eight-foot bottom. "Let's catch 'em while we can," he said.

Ginny and I pulled our tossle caps down over our ears, slung oilskin aprons around our necks, and wriggled into the oysterman's trademark—rubber gloves. By the time we had stationed ourselves at a waist-high board that spanned the boat amidships, Billy had piled several bushels of shells in front of us to be culled. Ginny and I set our hands churning legal oysters—larger than three inches from hinge to mouth —off the board and into the bottom of *Yankie*. Many of the oysters were grown together in clumps, so we worked with hammer-shaped chisels to break dead oysters and those smaller than three inches from the keepers.

The clap, clap, bang, bang of the hammers beat out an accompaniment for Billy's work. He stood on the gunwale near the stern of the boat and began weaving the long-leaf yellow pine shafts back and forth across his chest. The tongs at the bottom of the shafts scooped oysters into their jaws. Billy's body swayed with the rhythm of his arms and the sounds of the culling. He leaned into his work. His feet shuffled—half step ahead, back step, half step ahead, back step. He danced on the edge . . . then he moved forward to the culling board, where he raised the loaded tongs with a hand-over-hand motion and spilled the contents before Ginny and me.

For two hours we kept the beat, Billy danced, the radio chattered, and thousands of Canada geese and whistling swans stirred on shore. The air warmed. No one spoke.

At nine-thirty Billy Adams stopped and looked at the heap of oysters piled against the engine box. "How many do you guess, Gin?"

"Fifteen . . . I guess." They both laughed, as if Ginny's words had the magic of making a wish come true.

"OK, Cookie," said Billy.

Ginny produced coffee and sandwiches. We wiped oyster mud from our faces and ate. For the first time since *Yankie* had arrived on the bar, we noticed that three other boats had joined us.

As Billy ate his sandwich he called to an older waterman, lounging against his boat's cabin watching a young man picking through a heap of unculled oysters, "Sam, that fella thar just about as slow a culler as you are, ain't he?"

"Your mother," said the old man. He fired an oyster across the water past Billy's head.

A woman culler on another boat broke into a chuckle at the antics of Billy and his rival.

Billy gave her his shy grin: "Hey, Miss Sarah, you better look to who's laughin'. Old Cap'n Pete done snuck in the cabin for another snort o' mash."

The woman turned to discover that the man, who had been tonging just a moment before behind her back, had slipped into his boat's cabin where he was indeed drinking from something that looked like a pint of whiskey.

"Drunk!" she said.

The tonger beamed back at his wife, "This Bay ain't no place for a sober man."

"You old son of a . . ."

The crash of a load of oysters on *Yankie*'s culling board ended Ginny's and my laughter over the distractions of the morning. Billy danced on the gunwale faster than ever. We took up the cadence. Billy's arms moved in arabesques. *Yankie* filled with oysters.

A whining outboard engine broke the tune. "Here comes the man!" shouted a tonger. The man was one of the patrol officers for the Maryland Marine Police. His job was to make spot checks among the watermen to ensure that they were obeying oystering laws. As soon as Ginny Adams heard the patrol boat's engine she began muttering oaths. Ginny's complaints reflected 110 years of rivalry between watermen and the Marine Police. In 1868 the Oyster Navy, parent of the modern Marine Police, was to prevent skipjacks from poaching oysters from tongers' bars. Prior to World War I there was much shooting between watermen and Oyster Navy steam and sailing patrol boats as the government tried to force independent-minded oystermen to abide by conservation laws. As recently as twenty years ago some Marine Police boats carried machine guns mounted on their bows.

"Here comes Santa Claus, Gin," said Billy, as the patrol boat pulled alongside *Yankie*.

"You mean Scrooge," said Ginny. She turned to me: "Do you believe this rascal gave me a ticket last Christmas Eve? He picked through my pile for ten minutes till he'd found more than 5 percent of the catch were small oysters. Course the oysters were all grow'd together so a person had to miss culling some of the little ones, but that didn't matter to 'Mr. Lawman.' No, sir, he just handed me a thirty-dollar fine and said, 'I'll be wishin' you Merry Christmas.' Up his Christmas, I say."

Billy laughed at Ginny's fervor. "Law's the law, Gin. Don't pay to mess with it," said Billy, who winked at the patrol officer stepping aboard *Yankie*. The officer made a cursory inspection of the culled oysters. Ginny Adams folded her arms across her chest and gave the lawman a cold stare.

When he left *Yankie* with no complaints the patrolman said, "Now you take care, Miss Ginny."

"You, too, cousin."

The rhythm of tonging began again. The sun stood high in the south, and the next hour passed like a blue fall day. The tempo on *Yankie* gradually slowed. Ginny watched Billy massage his fingers, tong some more, then dangle his arms and shake them.

"Hurt?" she asked.

"Naw, just a little numb."

"Take your pills this morning?"

"They don't help, Ginny."

"Maybe the doctor could give you another shot of cortisone."

"Forget it," he said. "I got my limit. Let's go home. How many bushels you guess?"

"Thirty-five."

"Hope it's so."

I cleared the culling board and thought about Billy's "numb" hands and "his pills." I had heard the old men who hang out at the Phillip's station in Tilghman call this phenomenon "tonger's disease"—"It's all of 'em that got it, but none that's goin' to say it's so." I wondered what my ancestors had done before the invention of cortisone and amphetamines.

Yankie's engine started. Other tongers checked their watches—11:30. One of the tongers compared the piles of oysters in his fellow's boats to the pile in *Yankie* that looked much larger. "Billy's done it again, boys," he said. "He don't know that there's some of us that calls twenty bushels a full day's work!"

Billy just gave the other tongers his grin and turned *Yankie* toward home.

At the buyer's wharf both the tallyman and Ginny kept track of the amount of oysters unloaded from *Yankie*. Thirty-five bushels. Ginny collected more than $200 in cash and a receipt for the sale.

She took the receipt and added it to a collection of similar ones stashed in a shopping bag. "This is for the taxman," she said. "And this is for you." Ginny handed me $40 and pushed the rest of the cash into her jeans pocket.

"Hey, Ma," said Billy. "Ain't ya give me either dollar?"

Ginny chuckled and shoved Billy Adams up the wharf. "Come on, Mr. Adams, I know a stray lady that'd love to buy you lunch."

Billy turned to me. "Improved social life," he said. "Beats everything, even gunning with Junior Marshall."

I had to do some thinking before I understood that the term "gunning" was something like what they called "hunting" back in Pennsylvania. "Gunning" seemed very popular among the watermen: the guys on the *Ruby Ford* were always talking about "favorite spots," gunracks in pickups were full, and the twelve-year-old boys who lived next door to me had disappeared into the woods with shotguns every day after school in the winter. There had been headlines in local papers: "Gunning Accident Kills Two," "Youths Shot While Gunning." I hadn't paid much attention to the headlines, but when I thought about gunning, it seemed to me that watermen were making an awfully big production out of rabbit hunting. Perhaps, though, the watermen knew something I didn't, so I decided that if I ever met Junior Marshall I would see if I couldn't stir up the bushes with the man.

We met in the Court Street Pub in Easton. It was Friday night and I was with Bart, Bobby, and some other dredgers. We were looking for the heart of the evening. We shared a six-pack as we headed off Tilghman Island. The beer made the Ford pickup ride so easily that we found ourselves in front of a "fancy" Easton bar without recalling passing through St. Michaels at twice the speed limit. In the Court Street Pub I drank expensive beer because Bart ordered it. I tried to keep from staring too obviously at pretty women: it seemed a long time since I had seen so many attractive people. Their tweeds and cable knits made me feel suddenly out of place in jeans, turtleneck, and seaboots.

"Who let the drudgers in?" a gruff voice barked.

Bart and Bobby spun instinctively on their stools to meet their challenger. I followed suit and expected to be faced by a New York bouncer type. But there were no belligerent tongers in sight. Instead, I saw a short dark man of fifty poking an open hand into the first mate's right. The man's stocky frame was draped with an elegant plaid sports jacket, and he spun his free arm around the shoulder of Bart. He grinned at me.

"What you got here, Bobby?" said the man to *Ruby Ford*'s mate.

"New man, Junie."

"I can see that, ain't no old drudger'd wear his seaboots one second more that he had to. Don't he have a name?"

"We just call him . . .

I gave my name quickly.

"Lord, I thought I'd met every waterman on the Eastern Shore," said the small man.

"They call this burly-headed devil 'Junior' Marshall cause his real name's Marion," the mate said to me. The dredgers snickered.

"So it is," said Marshall smiling back, "and I come by it more legitimate than many a drudger I've met." He winked at me. "It's my daddy's name. Boy, you don't have the accent for a waterman."

I explained to Junior Marshall about being from Pennsylvania, about my believing my ancestors had been watermen, about enjoying work on the water.

Marshall laughed. "Can't say too much for your choice of friends, but your heart's in the right place."

He offered his hand.

"Careful," teased Bart. "Junie Marshall's the biggest damned storyteller in Talbot County." Marshall winked again, and everyone laughed.

The rest of the night was as smooth as the early evening drive from Tilghman. Junior Marshall told stories that stood in contrast to his elegant clothes: dredging tales, tonging tales, Marine Police tales, and Navy tales. I was impressed with the scope of Marshall's careers on the water (although he was now an electrician), but where did Billy Adams's comments about Junie Marshall's gunning trips fit in? When I asked the small man about gunning, Marshall had only two things to say: "It ain't rabbits we're shootin'," and "Bring your twelve-gauge to the Carpenter Street Tavern for five o'clock breakfast tomorrow!"

When I woke to the drone of the alarm I was still wearing my clothes from the night before. They would serve. I grabbed my dredging parka and started the drive to Carpenter Street. In my car was a Remington shotgun, a box of steel-shot cartridges, and a hunting license—all borrowed. I had not handled a shotgun in five years.

"Would you look at that?" I heard Junior Marshall's voice echo through the Carpenter Street's dining room. "Old Randy looks like a mannequin from the window of Abercrombie & Fitch . . . showing off the refugee look." I thought I heard people snicker. Marshall sat with an older man he called Jim. The men's eyes flashed awake and clear. Red paths of fresh shaves cut across their cheeks. The gunners were dressed completely in khaki. They made room for me at the table.

I stared into my coffee and ordered a double portion of eggs and sausage. Marshall ordered hot cakes. Jim ordered nothing. He drummed his right index finger softly on the table.

"Jesus Lord, Randy, you look more frazzled than my wife Bobbie did this mornin'. This ain't dredgin', boy. You got to have your wits about you or someone other than a goose is goin' to get killed."

I nodded. So that was the gunner's game—Canada geese. Later on I learned that the game might also have been snow geese, mallards, black ducks, or canvas backs. Along with Canada geese, these waterfowl have been favorite targets for hunters since white men introduced firearms to the Chesapeake. In 1977 more than 503,000 Canada geese, 14,000 snow geese, 26,000 mallards, 22,000 black ducks, and 49,000 canvas backs wintered on the Maryland shores of Chesapeake Bay. During the hunting season that begins about November 1 and ends in mid-January, 240,000 geese and 74,000 ducks were shot by Maryland gunners. These harvest figures make the Chesapeake one of the best waterfowl hunting areas in the United States. The upper Bay draws large numbers of migrating geese from Ontario and ducks from the Canadian prairie because the Bay's brackish water and marshes grow large quantities of favorite waterfowl foods like wild rice, smartweed, and wild millet.

In the Carpenter Street dining room Jim wanted to hear Junior Marshall's story, "What happened to Miss Bobbie?" Jim continued drumming his finger.

"Honey you should o' seen it," said Marshall. "Drug my gamebag out o' the garage an' threw it on the floor in the kitchen, you know, by my gun and all. It was about 4:30 or so. The old lady was fixin' me my first breakfast. Well, I'm eatin' some country ham and not payin' any attention to the world. Miss Bobbie's fryin' up some toast and she says, 'Hey, Marshall, what in God's name do you got in that dern old gamebag?' 'What do you mean, Ma?' I says. 'Just some old goose feathers I expect. Why, do it smell?' 'Goose feathers, my eye,' she says. 'Smell nothin'. It's crawled clean across the floor.' 'Well, I just imagine it has,' I said, 'and it'll be walkin' itself out to the truck next thing you know. Took me eight years to train that bag.'

"Well, I laid my eye on the bag a minute just to see what Miss Bobbie had dreamed up, and all of a sudden it just sort of leaped two or three inches and puffed up like a blow fish. And here come my hound dog, Ahab. He pounced that son of a bitch like it was a five-pound gander. The bag lets out one hell of a squeal; then so does Miss Bobbie. Damned if a mouse didn't bust out o' that bag and run 'neath the old lady's legs and lose itself behind the refrigerator. When Ahab saw it was a mouse, he lost interest, but Bobbie she jumped and lit up on the kitchen counter.

" 'Damn you, Junior Marshall,' she says, her breathin' hard and lookin' at me like she was crazy or drunk. 'We've been married thirty-five years and you ain't learned to take me seriously yet.' 'Well,' I says, 'I guess I best do it now. 'Cause if you don't come down from makin' a fool of yourself on that counter, the fried toast is goin' to burn and that might just ruin my day.' Damn, you believe she called me some perty names. That was one right frazzled woman."

Everyone in the Carpenter Street had been listening. They scored one for Junior Marshall.

Jim laughed less hard than most, "It's gettin' light, Junior; let's get packin' them cannons." He continued to drum his fingers.

"I hear ya," said Junior. "Don't want to rush the boy's meal. Want him wide awake 'fore he gets out on the water."

I said I was ready. I wondered privately what Marshall meant by "on the water."

When we went to load our gear in Marshall's truck, we found a huge Chesapeake Bay retriever waiting in the bed of the pickup.

"Damn, Ahab," said Marshall. "What in God's good name are you doin' here?"

"Believe he followed you from home, Junie," said Jim. "Old boy wants to go gunnin' is what it is!"

"That appears to be what he got on his mind, don't it? Well, it ain't gonna happen, dog. You're too damn old."

"In his second childhood, Junior."

"That must be it; he's fourteen years old for Christsake."

"One right smart retriever, though, weren't he?"

"That's no lie, but he's out to pasture now and don't know it. It's everytime I'm going gunnin' and try to leave him at home he pulls a stunt like this—stows away in the truck. Makes you want to take him along, but 'fraid he can't swim much any more. Jim, you can't swim neither stroke; that's bad enough. Why if the mess o' us got in trouble today we might spend the whole mornin' drownin' each other. I don't need that trash."

The gunners drove Ahab to the Marshall's house and locked the dog inside. Then the truck drove back a narrow road on the Bay Hundred Peninsula. Jim rapped his index finger on the dashboard of the truck.

The truck drove through the gate of an estate on a point surrounded by water. We stopped in front of a boatshed larger than most Tilghman homes. The two gunners didn't speak, but began ferrying guns, gear, and more than sixty decoys out to the end of the dock. Twenty years ago all of these decoys would have been carved from native pine. For much of the first half of this century wooden decoys were plentiful on the Chesapeake: they were the remnants of the large decoy collections owned by men who made a living market gunning before game laws were enforced. Now carved decoys are collectors items. Beautiful old decoys may sell for several hundred dollars, and decoy carving has become a cultivated folk art for display purposes. Today's decoys are made from styrofoam shaped in molds. Plastic geese cost gunners about five dollars apiece.

I picked up an arm-load of styrofoam decoys and tried to look as if all of this were old hat to me, but I had no idea where I was or what to expect next. Minutes later the gear was packed into a green aluminum outboard, and Marshall guided the boat out into open water. The grey streaks of dawn cut the eastern sky. As the dull light broke across the water I recognized familiar twists in the shoreline: this is where I had tonged oysters with Billy Adams—Broad Creek. A light breeze stirred the water. The air felt as warm as early fall. The outboard stopped.

"Get 'em out," said Junior Marshall as he uncoiled twenty-five feet of green anchor line from the neck of a decoy and threw the lead weight, anchor line, and decoy into the water.

Jim and I took up the task. Twenty minutes later the decoys were bobbing in a life-like cluster. Marshall used a paddle to maneuver the boat through a pack of decoys while Jim repositioned a few of the plastic geese that were too close to each other. Several times the boat rocked so much that it shipped water and Jim almost lost his balance.

Jim shot an annoyed glance back at Marshall, "We been gunnin' together forty years; you'd think we'd be able to keep from sinkin' this here boat."

"Yeah, Jim," said Junior Marshall, "but I been upset so many times sailin' my log canoe that tippin' over's beginning to seem the natural thing to do."

Jim didn't laugh. Neither did I. I remembered Bernard's stories about the killing cold in Bay water. I began to speculate about how dangerous it would be for all three men to shoot from this unstable boat.

The decoys were all in place. Junior started the motor. The boat turned toward shore. A cluster of evergreens sat in the creek about twenty-five yards downwind and inshore of the decoys. As the boat approached the thicket, I saw that the evergreens were laced around a wooden box mounted on pilings. It was a duck blind. I was relieved to know the blind, not the boat, was the platform for shooting.

Junior Marshall tucked the boat beneath a carport affair camouflaged by brush behind the blind. I secured the mooring lines and began unloading guns and ammunition through a hatch in the back of the blind just as if I had done it a thousand times. I was pleased that I had not betrayed my inexperience.

Once all three of us were in the drab green plywood blind, we closed the hatch behind us and began jockeying for position along the ten-foot bench seat. Jim had squatted into the windward corner of the blind as soon as he had climbed in. It seemed to me that Jim had commandeered the best position in the blind: I knew that birds land into the wind, so they would approach the decoys from Jim's side of the blind. He would have the best and longest view of any approaching targets. I headed for the leeward end of the blind hoping that if I missed a shot I could blame it on my position, but Junior Marshall spoke up.

"Get in between us, boy. Jim here has snookered me out o' Paradise so the hell with it. I'm goin' all the way down to leeward, stare at these goldplated, five-dollar-each decoys, and suck hind tit."

"Aw, Junior, I ain't tryin' . . . ," began Jim.

"Don't want to hear nothin' more about it," said Marshall. "I'll just sit down here t'other end and be glad I'm not the boy whose got to worry about whether it's your breath or your armpits that reek more."

"Um, hum, hum! Ain't he one common burly-headed sombitch," said Jim.

We laughed for a second, then we quietly removed shotguns from cloth cases and loaded three shells into the magazine of each gun. Marshall and Jim leaned their weapons against a rail in the front of the blind and sat back in their seats. After a few minutes Jim's finger began drumming on the side of the blind. Marshall farted loudly as if in retaliation: "Woo wee," he said, waving his hand in front of his face, "that was two sharp breakfasts I et."

An hour passed. The sky stayed grey. The temperature warmed so much that we peeled out of our jackets and sweaters. Not a goose appeared.

"Damned, if this ain't poor," said Jim.

"I knew it weren't goin' to be great guns," said Junior, "but I *did* expect to see a goose."

"Damn, it's hot."

"I know it is: it's even too hot for winter crabbin'. If it stays like this, them geese are like to go back to Canada."

"Listen!"

Guns sound.

"Down the creek."

"Where?"

"High sons of bitches. Over the point."

"Here they come."

We jumped to our feet to get a better view through the brush slits in the blind. Marshall and Jim pulled small wooden tubes from their breast pockets.

Haa—onk. Haa-onk. Honk. Honk. The gunners blew into their homemade goose calls. I watched Marshall try to "call down" the geese. He stood on his toes, but kept his knees bent as if he were ready to pounce on something just outside the blind. With each honk he blew from the call, Junior Marshall craned his neck in the direction of the flight of geese that were making a broad circle overhead. I stretched my neck, too, to follow the birds. The sounds of the goose calls seemed to duel with one another in the blind.

The geese began to honk back. They circled again. Junior and Jim's calls intensified. Suddenly the geese veered away from the blind and climbed over a corn field.

"Not like to come down for love or decoys in this heat," said Jim.

"Hell no," said Junior, "and there ain't a sky made grey enough not to reflect off Randy's forehead when he's pokin' it out of the blind that way. Where's your hat, boy? Ain't no damn goose stupid enough to pitch in front o' this here blind when he see's your head flashing like the full moon."

I mumbled something about forgetting my hat and sat quietly. Before this moment I had not thought about why Junior and Jim had been wearing long-billed, brown baseball caps.

"Here he come," whispered Jim.

"Where?"

"Down the creek. A single. See him? When I say now, Junior, you jump him."

I sat rigid in my seat. A bird set its wings to glide twenty-five yards to windward.

"Now!" whispered Jim.

Marshall sprung to his feet and shouldered his gun in one motion: "Damn you, Jim," burst Junior, dropping his aim. "You want me to gun down a good old black duck who won't be in season for another week? What you want—me to go to jail for gunning violation?"

"Just testing your reflexes. Didn't want you to get bored or nothin'," laughed Jim. He made a loud drum with his finger on the blind.

"Well, OK then, *don't* let me get bored, but *you* go to jail when the game warden shows up."

"When anyone ever get more than a fine for outlaw gunnin'?"

"Just you ask Red Floyd about that," began Marshall. Junior told the story of a wealthy country gentleman named Red Floyd. Floyd loved hunting fowl so much that he built a fresh water lake on his estate to attract game. Floyd even drilled a well to keep the lake filled with water. Marshall guessed the project cost more than $12,000. But apparently the lake was not enough to guarantee Floyd unlimited gunning, so Floyd began sprinkling corn in the pond as bait. Of course, gunning at Floyd's became remarkable, and the game warden noticed this phenomenon. Soon he began writing up Floyd and his friends for taking more than their bag limits. That didn't stop the violations. Hundred dollar fines meant nothing to men with Floyd's money. Finally, the frustrated game warden made a survey of the amount of corn found on the bottom of Floyd's pond. According to Marshall, Floyd was convicted of baiting fowl on the basis of fewer than one hundred kernels of corn found in an acre of pond bottom. The judge who convicted Red Floyd told the gentleman to expect six months in jail for his next offense.

"Ain't like them days when we used to catch forty, fifty, sixty ducks or some swans. Lot o' the old boys used to make a winter's livin' market gunnin'! No more."

"Yeah," said Junior, "those punt guns was the size o' cannons, some of 'em. Old fellas filled 'em with junk and glass. Bring down more birds than you could carry home. I remember Captain John. . . ."

Mid-morning arrived. The gunners marked it by the arrival of a tonger on an oyster bar 300 yards down the creek: "Must be nine o'clock. There's old fast Eddie come to catch his three bushels." The geese flew high. Jim and Junior passed the time by telling each other gunning stories they must have recited every winter season. One of their favorites was how they came by the use of this elegant blind.

Junior had struck up a friendship years ago with the owner of the estate that dominated the shoreline near the blind. The gentleman was a retired lawyer and Marine Corps officer from the Western Shore called Colonel Miller. The Colonel wasn't much of a gunner himself, but he enjoyed watching the Eastern Shoremen hunt fowl. An old waterblind had sat unused for years off Miller's property, and one day he offered it to Junior and Jim. After that, Junior and Jim had maintained and gunned the old blind. A tradition developed. The gunners would hunt the blind; the Colonel would watch through the picture window of his front porch. When the gunners were finished for the day the Colonel always invited them into his house to warm their bones in front of a fire and warm their spirits with hot buttered rum. I imagined the after-gunning sessions—long, rum-soaked, warm, and full of locker-room humor—from the comments of Jim and Junior: "Colonel Miller, he was one right old boy, slicker 'an goose grease."

Two years ago the old blind had collapsed and the Colonel had died leaving plans for "the best damned duck blind in Talbot County" on his desk. Junior and Jim had begun looking for new places to gun, but shortly after the Colonel's death, his widow approached the two gunners and asked their advice and direction in erecting the new blind. No expense was spared. Now the Colonel's widow watched the gunners from her picture window. Junior and Jim were quick to tell me Mrs. Miller was "one right lady, slicker 'an goose grease." And this was "one perty new blind," even if you just watched the breeze cut across the blue water, listened to the honking of distant geese, and talked away your life.

The honking grew louder.

"Where they at, Jim?"

"Coming down the creek. Lookin' good: a single and a pair. See 'em?"

Marshall nodded as he pushed his head part way through the brush of the blind and began honking on his goose call.

I sat still; I didn't want the reflection of the light on my forehead to spook the geese.

Jim drummed his right index finger on the bench seat fast, but quietly. The geese winged closer.

"Here they come."

"Don't shoot 'til they're within thirty-five yards," said Marshall.

"That's what they say about this steel shot," said Jim. "Cuts the killing range of a twelve-gauge to half what it used to . . ."

Pop, Poppop. The shots came from a blind 200 yards up the creek. One of the geese fell, the others veered sharply across the water.

"What the samhill?" said Marshall.

"Judas Priest, he got our gander."

"How'd he do that, Jim?"

"Don't know. Those birds was closer to us than to him. I know he wasn't obeying the law. Had to have lead shot to bring down the gander at that range. Probably one of those damn city gunners from Bal'mer using that blind."

"It was a nice shot, but I do believe I could have made it with lead."

"Wouldn't even try it with steel. It'd just tear 'em up a bit," said Jim.

"Honey," said Junior, "there ain't no sense in doin' that. This here new ruling that requires us to use steel shot on the Bay makes about as much sense as puttin' galoshes on a duck. The Feds, they say the geese eat lead shot and get poisoned by it. Maybe they do in shallow ponds and fields, but we're shootin' into fifteen feet of water. No goose goin' to find the shot what gets down there. Foolish rule. Yes sir. But wounding a bird is worse. Nothin' I want to do less than cripple a goose."

"That's the truth. If you hunt, you better kill a thing clean."

"And eat all the game you take. Damn, it makes me mad to see a goose killed for no reason. And crippled, well, I'll tell you about these city gunners. . . ."

Time passed. Jim and Junior reinforced each other's hunting ethics. They told themselves tales about how noble an animal a goose is—"Why I've seen ganders smarter than my son-in-law, and he teaches at the high school."

When the oysterman down the creek stowed his tongs and headed for home, Marshall said it was growing too late in the morning to be gunning. Jim and Junior began grumbling again. This time they complained about the "stupid" geese winging high overhead in tight formation.

Suddenly Marshall was on his feet crouching through the brush like an Indian. Honk, Honk. "Come down, you bitches." Honk, Honk. "This isn't the Berlin airlift, you know!"

Jim added his calls to the racket from the blind. Jim's index finger was twitching faster than ever. Honk, Honk.

Five geese, one arm of a vee formation, broke from one of the flights passing overhead. They began a wide descending circle over the decoys. I heard the geese as they turned behind the blind. They called loudly to the decoys. Jim and Junior called back.

"See 'em yet, Jim?"

"No—no—wait, here they come."

Honk, honk.

"Lookin' good?"

"I think they'll do it. Call 'em in."

Honk, Honk.

The flight of geese rounded the blind and turned upwind toward the decoys. The birds were only thirty feet off the water, a hundred yards downwind, and closing. Junior continued producing intermittent calls. Jim had already laid his right hand on his gun.

At fifty yards downwind the geese began to pitch their bodies diagonally as their wings stopped beating and spread to slow their flight and guide them into a landing. Junior and Jim shouldered their guns. The geese sailed toward the water on the outside edge of the decoys. They were at gun level almost in front of the blind, but still forty to fifty yards off.

I waited for Jim's right index finger to do its duty on the trigger at last, but instead I saw Jim glance at Junior.

The geese glided dead ahead.

Marshall glanced back at Jim.

Two more glances shot between the men.

Simultaneously they dropped their guns from their shoulders.

"Damn," yelled Marshall. The geese spooked. Their wings beat. They climbed away across the creek.

"Just about ten yards too far," said Jim.

"Might as well been a friggin' mile as far as my cannon's concerned," said Junior.

"Well the hell with it."

"You mean that, Jim?"

" 'Deed I do. It's too hot for gunnin'. Let's go home."

"You heard him," Marshall said to me. "I guess that right index finger of yours can stop twitchin' now, Jim. I allow the bet's off."

"Bet?" I asked.

Jim and Junior started to laugh. "Well, hell yeah, boy. Don't you Pennsylvanians always bet on who kills the first bird?"

"Right," I said, trying to cover my ignorance. We began unloading our guns.

After the decoys were retrieved and we were ashore, Colonel Miller's widow appeared on the porch of her manor house. Her waving arm made it clear that we were invited over to the house.

"Can't offer you a warm fire today," said a handsome woman in slacks and sweater.

"No, ma'm, we don't need it," said Jim.

"And guess we don't need geese," said Junior.

"Empty handed?" asked the lady.

"We just decided that there weren't no sense shootin' geese 'til this warm spell passes," said Junior. "Hell, it's like to crabbin' weather now. Don't believe a man should touch an arster or a goose, do you, Ma'm?"

"Well, I guess not. But I didn't even hear you fellows take a shot."

"Neither shot," nodded Junior. "You might say it's safer that way for all concerned—geese and Pennsylvanians."

Cold Weather

veryone's water pipes froze the day before Christmas on Tilghman Island. The wind blew northwest at forty knots. No one went oystering. Watermen gathered inside Gary's Phillips 66 station that faces Knapps Narrows. They paid twenty cents to make their own instant coffee and lean against shelving stacked with marine supplies ranging from oilskins and life preservers to bilge pumps and motor oil.

Bart Murphy was one of the many islanders who passed the hours from sunrise to midmorning at Gary's. He ate TastyKakes and shifted from one foot to the other in the front room of the Phillips station. I stood nearby listening to Bart talk with the other captains.

"They say there's ice a man can walk on up to San Domingo Creek."

"One more week o' this cold weather and them St. Michaels tongers like Billy Adams may as well go to Florida for the winter."

"Gonna be a mess a' boats that don't leave the dock till March."

" 'Fraid it's so. Ain't seen cold weather like this since '34."

" 'Member old Dutch Harrison and some boys took his truck out on the ice and cut holes over Bunker Hill oyster bar."

"They dropped dredges through the holes and towed 'em with the truck, didn't they?"

"Could be either day now, we'll see Bart doing the same thing."

"Liable to," said Bart. "Ain't made enough to go to Florida, yet."

"Don't ya just bet if it comes to towing dredges from a pickup truck, the state's gonna up and say it's illegal 'cept on Monday and Tuesday when they 'low the dredge boats to run under power?"

"Believe those sonuvabitches might do just that, but that won't stop ole Black Bart, will it?"

Bart Murphy ran his hands through his hair a number of times: "Believe we'd just rig a squaresail to the truck, or maybe put some iceboat runners and a sail on one o' these little tongin' skiffs. But I hope it don't come to that. I'm poor enough as it is."

"Hold it, Cap'n Bart. You get either one of us dredgers beat so far this season. The tallyman says you been catchin' 600 bushels a week. With buyers paying $9 a bushel, I reckon you got $5,000 in the bank already."

"Don't have hardly a lick," said Bart. "Replaced a lot of bottom plankin' in the *Ruby Ford* this fall. Boatyard's 'bout dollarin' me to death."

"That's how come you bought your oldest girl a new car, I guess."

Bart's smile dropped from his face. Up to this point he had been enjoying the jibes and the conversation. It had been relaxing him, but now his arms tensed and his jaw muscles set into bulges beneath two-days growth.

"That girl deserves everything I can give her," said Bart Murphy. "Sixteen years old and she spent the whole summer, almost seven days a week, crabbin' with me. Not many girls would do that."

"There's some that don't do nothin' but hang out down to the park and wait for the boys to whistle. Common sluts."

"It's the way it'll always be. Not much to do but follow the water and have a family on this island."

"Ain't it the truth. I told my kids to work hard in school, so's they could go to college. 'Least join the service and get off this island. Told 'em there's no good sense in followin' the water. But not one of 'em got farther than St. Michaels, and she married a waterman."

"Guess we just all ate so many arsters and crabs, they run in our blood."

"Well, I wish they'd run in my water pipes," said Bart Murphy. "Four girls and a baby's in that house and there ain't a bit of water. Gonna be some Christmas if this weather don't thaw."

"Guess I better run up to St. Michaels and get the plumber. Nothin' gettin' done hangin' here," said one man.

"You're right," chorused a group of young watermen. "Best roll over to town and finish shoppin'. See what's doin' at Carpenter Street and the Quarter Deck."

The men turned their trucks inland across Knapps Narrows drawbridge. It was 10:30 in the morning.

By noon most of the water pipes on Tilghman Island thawed. Women worked at preparing geese and hams for family feasts. Children helped their mothers. Men swarmed through St. Michaels in pickup trucks, and there was standing room only at the Quarter Deck and Carpenter Street saloons. The watermen had finished all their Christmas Eve chores.

Carols rang from the church tower in St. Michaels and the jukeboxes in the taverns. Windows and watermen steamed in the heavy air of beer and smoke. Dredgers from skipjacks called *Sigsbee*, *Robert L. Webster*, *Stanley Norman*, *Lady Katie*, and *Kathryn* pressed shoulder to shoulder with tongers named Hadaway, Harrison, Spurry, and Messick. No one paid for his own drinks.

Billy Adams held his place at the Carpenter Street bar; Bart Murphy sat beside him, telling Billy about just buying a movie camera to take pictures of his two-year-old son, Bart, Jr.—the son the skipjack captain had been waiting for since the day he married. "Boy'll be tough enough for drudgin' next season," said Murphy.

49

"Could be, Bart. I've heard he's feisty enough now to break the eyeglasses of your ole' daddy," said Billy.

"Boy did do it, but my father told Lil' Bart to give him a punch. Can't blame a kid for doing what he's told, can you?"

"That don't last long," said Billy, "doin' what they're told."

"Little Billy giving you trouble?"

"Awh, hell no, Bart. That kid's good as they come. He just don't listen any more than I did when I was eighteen. 'Join the service,' I tell him. 'Learn a trade,' I tell him. What's he do?"

"Tonging with Ginny's father, I heard."

"You heard right. And he's grow'd his blond hair down his back. Knows his mother and I hate it." Billy laughed and shook his head.

"Boy's 'bout as stubborn as his old man. Believe he'll be just as good a waterman, too," said Bart.

"Well, I guess there's worse he could do. Some of these young fellas have messed up their lives right bad on drugs and things. That ain't little Billy, thank God."

"Hell, Billy," said Bart. "Look at it this way: Lil' Billy was born with a pair of oyster tongs in his hand. He's got eighteen years headstart on Randy here, and ole Randy's hair's just as long as Lil' Billy's."

I frowned in disagreement. After two months of dredging, I had learned that a crewman doesn't talk back to his captain. I had heard captains threaten stubborn crewmen with a shove overboard, and I had seen a skipper go after a crewman with a swinging shovel.

Both Billy Adams and Bart Murphy seemed to sense what I was thinking. The older men laughed and rapped me on the shoulders.

"Cheer up, boy," said Bart. "We ain't about to cut anyone's hair."

"Hell, no," said Billy. "It's Christmas."

Junior Marshall passed through the afternoon revelry at Carpenter Street long enough to swill several Black Labels and invite half of the tavern's occupants to an open house he and his wife Bobbie were having that evening. Bart and Billy pledged their attendance, claiming they had no use for a rascal like Junior, but they'd be obliged to come "just for Miss Bobbie's sake."

The night was more of the same. Men talked louder and drank faster. The partying continued, but the location shifted to different barrooms and private homes on Bay Hundred. The Marshall's party, where 150 people banqueted on country ham, was only one stop in a movable feast. At each party people heard Bart Murphy tell about having to kill his bird dog and pay twenty-two dollars in damages because the hound had broken into a neighbor's chicken coop and eaten some poultry. The chicken owner had asked Bart to pay just for damages, but Bart said the dog had to be destroyed too—"Once a young bird dog got the taste o' chicken blood he ain't good for nothin' except causing trouble." But Bart's son loved the dog, so the skipjack captain was circulating St. Michaels in search of a new puppy for little Bart—"Boy's nearly three years old, got to have a dog." The search and parties ran into the twilight hours of the morning. Wives and children were nearly ready to wake for Christmas when the men came home. Before going to bed, Bart Murphy piled an old blanket on the floor of his truck. He guessed the blanket would be enough to keep Little Bart's new puppy warm until breakfast.

Tilghman Island was surrounded by ice when the watermen finally woke to their breakfast calls. Some men checked the freezing temperature and pulled into long underwear and work clothes before they remembered that it was Christmas and they need not fight the icefloes this morning.

I didn't know how watermen felt about Christmas so I paid

a morning visit to my captain. At the Murphy's, I saw Bart present his son with a seven-week-old half-Chesapeake, half-bird dog bitch. Within seconds Little Bart had named his new pet after the old chicken eater, Jack. The boy rolled on the floor of the living room with the puppy. The Murphy girls watched as their father recorded Little Bart's third Christmas with the movie camera purchased on Christmas Eve. For the Murphy girls, Christmas was traditional: gifts of new clothes, presents for their pet goat and pony, then kitchen work to prepare for relatives who would arrive by noon. I didn't mention work to my captain; I offered a Christmas greeting and took my leave.

I saw the Marshalls arrive on Tilghman in late morning with their car filled with presents and food. Junior and Bobbie Marshall said they had a gathering of the clan planned, and they had been getting ready for it every since they had cleared the house of the Christmas Eve party and roused the guests who had stayed the night. Now they had come to Tilghman Island to share the holiday with no fewer than thirty-five of their relatives.

"You may as well join us. You're probably related to the whole bunch. Come on, boy, there'll be no working until these watermen get Christmas and family out of their blood, and that's some days off."

I thanked Bobbie for the invitation, but I took the opportunity of a few days off to get back to my own family in Pennsylvania. As I left Bay Hundred I stopped for some coffee in St. Michaels. I met Billy Adams and asked how Christmas was.

"Best," said Billy. "When I finally got up this morning what handsome thing do you think I seen sitting across the breakfast table from me and Gin? First I says to Gin, 'That's no one I know.' She says, 'Look harder, Billy.' You know what it was I saw? It was Li'l Billy with a haircut, that's what. Done it for his mother and me. You know, for Christmas."

When I returned from Pennsylvania, I found five inches of snow in Tilghman, giving the island its first white Christmas season in a decade. After a few warm days ashore with my family, I wasn't certain I wanted to go dredging again. However, back in November I had made a promise to myself to investigate my ancestry. I had not yet fulfilled my promise so I reported to the wharves as usual for a morning of dredging. There the shipjack crews were engaged in snowball fights. I joined the chaos and fought several skirmishes before Bart Murphy called us to rig the push boat and cast off the *Ruby Ford*'s lines.

As the skipjack plowed into the Choptank River, the crew watched Bernard fry eggs, sausage, and grits in the cabin. The men listened to the chatter on the marine radio: watermen repeated storm warnings—winds northwest at eighteen to twenty-five knots this morning, increasing above thirty-five knots this afternoon, gale warnings in effect after 0900—and passed on hearsay about trees and power lines being blown down on the western shore of the Bay. Someone noted that this was the same weather forecast he had heard three weeks before when the skipjack *F. C. Lewis, Jr.* had capsized off Kent Island.

"Blew ninety knots, they say."

"Waves rolled her over without a lick o' sail on her."

"Them fellas was hanging onto the boat's high side for nearly twenty minutes 'fore the *Helen Virginia* could get to 'em."

"I heard they got that boat rigged to go dredging again."

"Got divers to refloat her the same day of the storm. Took her back home down the Bay at the end of the week."

"She pulled into Dogwood Cove up to Tilghman yesterday."

"Goin' drudgin'—likely to be sailin' with us today."

"I would have lost my nerve if I was them boys."

"Yes, sir, I believe that would a' killed me for drudgin'."

We ate breakfast and remembered the Baltimore *Sun*'s account of the *F. C. Lewis*'s accident:

> Annapolis (Special)—A Deale Island skipjack capsized in high winds and cold, choppy waters while its crewmen were dredging for oysters just south of the Bay Bridge about 10:30 A.M. today, the Maryland Natural Resources Police reported.
>
> All six crewmen from the *F. C. Lewis* were immediately rescued by a nearby skipjack, the *Helen Virginia*. No injuries were reported.
>
> Authorities said the cause of the capsizing was not immediately determined, but they indicated the choppy weather may have been a factor.
>
> Divers and a tug boat were en route to the scene from Baltimore to right the overturned vessel, which was reported still afloat when Marine Police arrived on the scene minutes after the incident.

Ruby Ford's deck was deep in snow. After breakfast I began shoveling the stuff overboard and trying to figure out if Bart was as apprehensive about the weather reports as I was. The only concern that the captain showed was to bend periodically from his post at the wheel and reach into the cabin to turn up the volume of the boat-to-boat CB conversation. I kept shoveling. Before Bart Murphy ever gave the call to hoist sail, I knew he was planning to hide from the strong winds by dredging an oyster bar near the leeward side of Tilghman.

Ruby Ford and other boats had been here—Bunker Hill—a lot this winter, and there weren't many oysters left. I prepared for a twelve-hour day; I placed three pairs of rubber gloves to warm in the galley oven.

As the crew set the full sails on *Ruby Ford*, Bernard nudged me: "Cheer up and look at that," he pointed to the fleet of skipjacks tacking against a background of snow-covered cottages and fir trees on Tilghman. "Ain't seen neither a purtier day than this in all my years of drudging. Seems like Christmas, snow, and sailboats is a thing o' the past. Believe I won't see 'em altogether again. Like to stop time, ya know?"

I did, but I couldn't put off the banging of the dredges on the side of the boat that called me to my knees for hours of sorting oysters, ducking spray, and shielding my eyes from the snow that chopped visibility to less than a quarter mile.

"Them drudges is swimming off the bottom," called the captain, as the *Ruby Ford* charged across the surf faster than I had ever seen her move. "Get that canvas off her."

The crew fixed two reefs in the sails; but the dredges were still being pulled too fast to drag evenly over the oyster bar. The seas continued to build—perhaps five-feet high, in short intervals. *Ruby Ford*'s mast swung in a wide arc, as the waves hit her broadside. I joined the other crewmen who held on to the frames of the winding machine. We tugged the dredges toward the middle of the deck to prevent them from washing away. *Ruby Ford*'s bow dove under water and deep foam raced over the decks. For several seconds the skipjack paused with her hull almost completely submerged beneath the Bay. The crew clung to anything that would support them.

"Bobby, Ray, Ronnie, get the push boat rigged. Charlie Buck, drop that jib. Now!" The captain barked his men into action as soon as the skipjack's decks rose above the water.

"Randy, stand by that main halyard. Move, boy." Murphy fought his vessel's wheel with both hands.

As some of the crew secured the push boat astern and the mate ducked waves to start its engine, a scream came from the bow, "Hard to starboard, Cap'n!"

Murphy turned the boat to his right thirty degrees before he saw a skipjack tear out of the blizzard and nearly sideswipe the *Ruby Ford* as it charged past in the opposite direction. We stared blankly across three feet of water as the *Kathryn* swept past. Her crew gave us a look that asked, "How the hell did you guys get there?"

Then a gust hit *Ruby Ford*. Everyone's eyes fixed on the mast bowed under the strain of too much mainsail.

"Get sail off her, Goddamit all!" yelled Murphy as he turned the skipjack's bow into the wind and brought a sea ripping over the decks. Bernard and I pulled the mainsail part of the way down; then we threw our arms around the mast. When the roller passed, we tugged the sail all the way down; I hoped the push boat's engine was strong enough to drive *Ruby Ford* in these seas.

The Cadillac beat steadily from astern; between waves the crew furled the sails to prevent the gale wind from dragging the expensive dacron overboard.

With the sails off, *Ruby Ford* made slow but stable progress into the wind toward Knapps Narrows. It seemed that it had taken only a matter of seconds to secure the gear on the deck of the boat after the sails were down. I climbed into the cabin to pull off my soaking hat. Bits of ice clung to my eyebrows and ears. I shivered. Bobby began to take off his soaked clothes.

"Leave 'em on," said Bernard, as he passed out mugs of steaming coffee. "It's the only way you'll keep your body heat."

We followed Bernard's advice. The mate swore, "Damned, I thought we were drowned that time."

"See'd you hanging onto that mast, Bernard, like it was your old lady."

"Damn right; I'm too old for this nonsense."

"Then give it up, man."

"Give up your tail feathers; what I know but drudgin'?"

The men began to shiver less. We laughed: "Fuckin' drudgin' insanity."

On deck, Bart Murphy steered the boat toward home. Snow froze to his wet snowsuit. As the boat got closer to Tilghman Island, the wind and the seas eased quite a bit. Bart wiped the ice from his face with a towel passed up by the crew. He sipped coffee.

"Don't you boys freeze down there," he called to the crew in the cabin. The captain's teasing remarks provoked enough guilt to make us sit silently until *Ruby Ford* entered the Narrows.

Buck Garvin, the oyster buyer, met the *Ruby Ford* as she began landing her oysters. He paced the wharf, shielding his ears from the blizzard with gloved hands. Buck smiled at us.

"Boys, I don't know what you fellas is made of. Shame you let a couple of snowflakes scare you home."

"I ain't seen you out there, Cap," said Bobby.

"Ain't that dumb," said Garvin, ducking the barrage of snowballs that flew his way from *Ruby Ford*.

A fact of the day was this: we had caught only forty bushels of oysters; any factory job would pay more. Another fact: the temperature had already dropped to fifteen degrees and was supposed to fall to five degrees over the next three days. Bart Murphy was sorry; he told his boys to stay home until we got some decent weather. Some of us might find work tending bar, some would file for unemployment, some were too proud.

Watermen say that it's weather like this that holds their average reported net income below $10,000 per man per year. But bad weather may not tell the whole story. In 1976, more than 17,800 people worked as Chesapeake watermen in Maryland's portion of the Bay. In 1940, only 5,981 men had held licenses to harvest Maryland's Bay. National Marine Fisheries statisticians point out that 13,000 Maryland watermen were part timers in 1976: they earned less than half of their income on the Bay. Nevertheless, it seems likely from the growth in numbers of watermen over the past thirty-six years that fishing efforts have increased significantly while the annual harvest has remained about 55,000,000 pounds of seafood per year.

The statistics imply that the watermen's relative poverty grows from an increased fishing effort and a relatively stable harvest. But few watermen I know believe the implications of the statistics. When watermen do not blame the weather for hard times, they often turn on seafood processors around the Bay and buyers who daily ship fresh Chesapeake fish to wholesale markets in New York, Philadelphia, Washington, and Baltimore. Watermen claim that processors and buyers conspire to set prices paid to watermen at artificially low levels. The processors and buyers counter by saying that watermen make more money than they admit—that watermen have ways of hiding their earnings from the government. State and federal commerce and fisheries officials say that it is impossible to get a clear economic profile of the Chesapeake fisheries: almost no one in the business opens his books to the public—even when the market and the weather are bad.

When the gale let up, the Choptank River was frozen over and a barrier of ice several miles wide grew around the Bay-side of Tilghman. On the island, cars full of teenagers paraded back and forth past the fire hall and park. Young boys peppered the cars with snowballs. Occasionally the cars stopped each other and exchanged passengers or cans of beer before continuing to patrol the island. Almost no one else moved.

After days of watching this from the front room of Gary's Phillips station, I decided that I had been idle long enough. It was time to find out what I could about my heritage.

My first visit was to eighty-year-old Ada Harrison, who was Bobbie Marshall's mother and one of four widowed Harrison matriarchs whose homes lined the road to the Devil's Island section of Tilghman. "M'Ada," as people called Mrs. Harrison, overwhelmed me. She looked much younger than I had expected: her thin figure and sharp eyes fit a woman half her age. Before I realized that I was being led, M'Ada had me sitting in her living room with a cup of coffee in one hand and fresh pound cake in the other.

"I've been wondering when you'd come over for a visit," M'Ada told me. "Bobbie, my daughter, has told me all about you. Course, I've seen you around the island; new person's easy to spot."

"You know why I've come," I said. "You probably knew the first day you saw me on the island."

"I can't say I haven't thought about it. I've seen the look before: you aren't the first that's ever come back to follow the water. Dutch, my husband, used to say every fall that either day we'd see some poor soul come to find a job on the water. They'd show up as regular as the geese, and Dutch would swear every one of 'em was a relative."

"I don't want to bother you," I began.

"Lord, you aren't bothering me. Haven't I seen enough

Eastern Shore men that I know they can't help themselves? There's no cure for Choptank River water in your veins. You're gonna follow the water and drink whiskey and spend the rest o' your life wondering why. You got watermen's blood."

"Then it's always been this way?" I asked.

"I believe so. I came to this island in 1906 from my family's farm out on Poplar Island, and it seemed to me that the watermen I met back then acted like they had owned Tilghman for a thousand years."

"You don't sound like you think the watermen have a right to dominate this island."

"Now, I didn't say that, boy. I married a waterman and give birth to enough of them. I got to love them, but I'm still something different. I'm a Sinclair and my grandfather was part Choptank Indian. That information didn't used to be too popular among a lot of Tilghman Islanders. Maybe it reminded them that my grandfather held a prior claim on this island. Watermen weren't always Europeans."

For another hour M'Ada Harrison and I tried unsuccessfully to connect my family, who settled the Susquehanna Valley, with the Tilghman Island families who worked their way up the Bay toward Pennsylvania as schooner captains and boatbuilders. M'Ada insisted there was probably a link somewhere "way back," but I might have better luck searching church records. She was sorry she couldn't help me more.

Our conversation shifted to island traditions. M'Ada Harrison reminisced about living on Poplar Island at the turn of the century. She recalled that the island was much larger than it is now—"why there were twenty-six farms out there then"—and M'Ada marveled how her old homestead had become a hunting retreat for FDR and his cronies during the thirties: "For a while Poplar Island was famous, now no one but ghosts live there; before you're gone that old island's goin' to vanish beneath the Bay like Sharps Island."

There was a touch of resentment in M'Ada Harrison's voice as she talked about the Bay. She seemed to see the Chesapeake as something seductive, yet overwhelming and cruel. She had seen the Bay wash away large portions of familiar landscape. More than half of the 500 acres M'Ada knew in her youth as Poplar Island have washed away. In 1848 Sharps Island, off the southern end of Tilghman, contained 438 acres. By 1900 the island had eroded to 91 acres, and in 1953 it disappeared. Until recently Tilghman's western shore has eroded away at the rate of ten-feet per year. Despite bulkheads that have been erected to protect the island, further land loss is likely. The water level of the Bay continues to rise annually due to siltation from the Susquehanna River feeding the Bay head.

The old woman told me she had seen the Bay claim more than land. She told me about a Memorial Day Service held in Tilghman. Instead of just paying tribute to the war dead, the islanders gathered to honor fourteen Tilghman watermen lost on the Bay. M'Ada didn't go to the service—"It was sad, you know; I give up too many that I loved." She said her sister went: "Woman lost her husband and her son a few years back. They found her husband's crabbing skiff drifting east of Tilghman. Husband's watch was sittin' on the engine box and the engine was still running, but they never found the man. Must have fallen overboard and got left behind. That's the danger of working alone, but lots o' fellows with big families can't afford to share crabbin' money with a crew." M'Ada's nephew drowned the same winter when his oyster boat sunk. The bay had frozen him stiff in minutes.

This was not the kind of lore that I liked hearing, and I saw that the subject had made M'Ada uneasy, too. Maybe it was the bitter weather that made our conversation take its dark turn. I excused myself.

M'Ada Harrison's home faced Dogwood Cove where twelve skipjacks were iced in. When I left M'Ada's I walked over to some watermen huddled on the deck of one of the dredge boats; I was curious to see if they were planning to break out of the harbor.

"Gonna break some ice?" I called.

Three watermen turned and stared at me. Wrapped in hooded parkas, their faces looked blue. They didn't speak.

I repeated my question. Maybe the wind had blown the sound of my voice away. I had still heard nothing from the watermen, so I walked over the their vessel.

Finally, one man spoke, "Ain't December 7th is it?"

"What?" I didn't understand what the date had to do with going oystering.

"Ain't Pearl Harbor Day, is it?" asked the man.

"No," I answered.

"Then, believe we're goin' to try to go out." The watermen turned back to some tinkering around the skipjack's winding machine.

I stared at the vessel a moment longer; I was still puzzled by the waterman's reference to December 7. Then I saw the vessel's name lettered on the bow—*F. C. Lewis, Jr.* I remembered. Pearl Harbor Day was when the *Lewis* had capsized.

M'Ada Harrison's dialogue with me had included the name Sam McQuay. The name had surfaced before. McQuay was a boat carpenter who learned the trade from John B. Harrison of Tilghman, perhaps the best known builder of traditional Chesapeake workboats during the early twentieth century. McQuay had once almost built a crabbing boat for Bart Murphy, and he was now working on rebuilding Junior Marshall's racing log canoe, *Rover*. M'Ada Harrison told me to visit McQuay—"If it's Tilghman Island you got to know about, well, Sam's got some stories he can tell."

Sam McQuay worked in a boatshed in the village of Wittman across Broad Creek from Tilghman Island. I found McQuay sawing a piece of rotten bottom from a yellow hull that ran the length of the boatshed's interior. When I entered the shed, McQuay, a big man in his late sixties, shut off his Skilsaw and gave me a glare through thick glasses. I quickly introduced myself as a member of Bart Murphy's crew and as a friend of the Marshalls'.

McQuay laughed, "Oh, you're the new man."

I was bit startled to learn that news of my existence had carried to McQuay.

Without letting me speak, Sam McQuay assumed he had accurately identified me and continued talking: "You sure got yourself mixed up with a couple of good bastards. This here's Junie's log canoe I'm trying to chink together for him. Pain in the ass, just like its skipper."

I smiled. I wasn't sure how to react.

"You think you're related to people down here?"

I shrugged my shoulders. I was hoping . . .

"Could be you're related to John B. Harrison himself. Best damn boat builder in the world. Married his daughter. Man built boats no one else could figure out. There's no log canoe ever built that can outrace his *Jay Dee* and *Flying Cloud*. You know the old story about the *John B. Harrison*, don't you?"

I shook my head. I had never seen a log canoe before this afternoon. I had thought log canoes were small dugouts, but the hull lying on this boatshed floor was as big as that of many tonging boats.

"The log canoes were racing up at Claiborne. John B. was tending foresheet on the *Harrison*. On the way back from

Bloody Point the wind died and the canoe's crew wanted to put squaresails up on top of the masts, but Mr. Harrison told those boys to hold off. He said that pretty soon they were going to see a puff that would blow your nose off. But the boys finally convinced Mr. Harrison to let them set the squaresails. Well, when the squall hit the *Harrison* she flew ahead of all those other canoes and those boys on her begged to take the sails off. They were in the middle of Eastern Bay and afraid of capsizing. Weren't one of them able to swim.

"Well, John B. said the sails were staying on. 'Let her blow 'em off if she can,' said the old man. By this time people in Claiborne had seen the canoe coming and hundreds of them went down to the beach to watch; they'd never seen a sailboat go that fast. People say that when she hit the beach, her speed drove her a full five boatlengths up onto the sand."

McQuay looked me in the eye, "Now, tell me, don't you think that Mr. John B. Harrison knew how to make a boat that could go like the wind?"

I agreed. "Could John B. Harrison be my ancestor?"

"Lord, boy, how should I know? If you ain't related to him, you must want to be. John B. was some smart. Look here."

Sam McQuay led me around the boatshed, showing special boats, masts, and oars that John B. Harrison had built or that McQuay had copied from the Harrison design. I didn't quite understand all the technical things McQuay explained, but I gathered the story of how Sam had modeled his own life after the master shipbuilder who had taught McQuay the secret of log canoes.

"Mr. John B. could tell you some stories," said McQuay, as he began retelling bits of Tilghman Island myths. I heard tales of an annual pig slaughter and party that the men of Tilghman used to hold on Sharps Island, and of how the owners of the Sharps Island Hotel had bred all the black women servants to a "big black buck from Baltimore each fall" to replenish the labor force.

McQuay went to work with a mallet and chisel, cutting away more rotten wood from Junior Marshall's canoe but the carpenter didn't chase me away.

"So what do you think of Bart Murphy?" asked the carpenter.

I said I thought Bart was a good captain.

"I respect Bart Murphy," said the boatbuilder. "He and I had our differences about a crab boat I was supposed to build for him, but that's over. Give Bart credit; he started with nothing. He does right well, now."

"He does when the Bay isn't frozen over," I said.

"Yes, but it ain't like the old days when Bart's father, Wade, got his boat stove up in the ice. Old Cap'n Wade was a bastard. He'd be on my back in a minute if I didn't fix his boats when he tore 'em up. Told him once if he didn't let me alone, I'd take a hatchet to him—kill the son-of-a-bitch. That's how we used to talk back then; we thought we were tough—some of us were.

"God, one time Wade called me down to his drudge boat —he always had these worthless wrecks—and he showed me two mattresses he had stuffed in a hole in the bow. I says, 'Cap'n Wade, I think this old boat's a gonner.' He says, 'Shsss. I told the crew that a rat chewed through.' Well, the boat was rotten as hell, and he had just busted her up on thick ice. I says, 'Must have been a goddamn elephant rat.' When that nigger crew heard me, they jumped ashore faster than you could throw a line.

"I'll tell you, there's some nutty things that goes on out to that Island. Superstitious? Jesus, you know that no watermen will go out on the Bay in a boat painted blue, but did you know there's some that won't leave Tilghman wharf if a black walnut shell or leaf falls on their boat? I've seen men turn back if three crows flew across their bow. Yes, sir, just right back to the dock. Like black cats, I guess. I don't put no stock in it, but I may have had some bad luck from a black cat. You never know.

"Old Doc said he found me settin' on the edge of my grave this summer—ruptured gall bladder. Ain't that something? Could have been a black cat done it. You never know about death."

Still no work. New Year's Eve came with a zero-degree temperature and high winds. Even the teenagers on Tilghman stayed indoors. I huddled in front of a kerosene space heater all day reading about the habits of mallards, canvasbacks, brants, Canada geese, and whistling swans. It was even too cold for gunning. I waited for the dark. New Year's Eve was supposed to be a special night for watermen.

Sometime after sunset a horn blared outside my house. A car's engine revved and headlights flashed off and on. The car sat in the middle of the lawn. It was Bobby and some of the other men from the *Ruby Ford*. I joined the crew in a small camper mounted in the bed of a pickup. Inside, two men and three women warmed themselves with a propane heater and a communal bottle of whiskey.

"Ain't too cold, is it?" asked one of the dredgers.

"You must be kidding; seems like Alaska."

"Nothing like how old Peter must feel." The waterman, Tommy, spoke to one of the women. I had never seen her before.

The young woman forced a smile. Her face looked pretty and pale.

I didn't understand Tommy's remark.

He explained: "Sophie's husband Peter's crew on a St. Michaels tug. Been away on tows for near a month."

"Beats drudgin' for hardship, doesn't it?" said one of the other women.

"You get by," said Sophie, dryly.

Tommy spoke up, "Believe it might improve marriage."

"Not to you," said Sophie.

Tommy lost his voice. He drank.

I asked when Peter was due home.

"Yesterday," said the wife.

"It's ice slowed him down. Be in anytime," said one of the women.

"Ice got us all. Has to clear soon," I said.

"I'm ready." Sophie sipped whiskey, passed the bottle on.

"It's that kind of night, is it?" asked one of the women.

"For drinkin'," said a waterman.

"For waitin'," said a woman.

"And a thaw," added another voice. It was not Sophie's. She stared out the window at crusted snow.

The pickup rolled through Tilghman. The bottle passed. I had no idea what I was getting myself into.

The first stop was at Bart and Florence Murphy's house. Bobby and his wife, who had been in the cab of the pickup, led the crew into the captain's house. The new arrivals combined with the five Murphy children, new toys, puppy, and a Christmas tree to usurp all of the space in the tiny living room.

"C'mon Bart," said Bobby. "We've got to go up the road. Goin' to get down and dance tonight." The mate clapped his hands and did an Elvis Presley wiggle.

Florence Murphy passed bottles of Michelob around the room. Bart remained stationed in his easy chair beneath an oil painting of him at the wheel of the *Ruby Ford*. The captain shook his head and gave a bewildered smile. "I see right well the kind o' evening you got planned. Believe it's not tame enough for me." Bart winked and pulled his son onto his lap.

"C'mon, Florence," chorused a couple of the women.

"I don't think I will. Bart can go if he wants. Might have fun, but I'm not much for a party when Bart isn't working."

"Whose goin' to pay for all this, Bobby?" asked the captain. "There is some of you fellas that's already behind. Be that way all winter: pay you $500 on a Friday, and you come to me on Monday for a $100 advance—C'mon Cap', just let me have some 'til the end of the week. Lord, I hear it all season. Come March you won't have a penny to your names."

"Damn, Bart, you know how it is. You been up the road 'fore." The mate teased the captain. No one else would have dared.

Murphy began to laugh: "It's unhealthy to hang with you folks. Go on out of here 'fore you land me in trouble. Man's crew'd like to ruin his homelife, certain."

"Peace, Bart," said the mate. "We'll just leave you to listen to the gospel service on the radio . . . or whatever."

"Yeah, or whatever," the captain shot a grin at his wife.

As we prepared to leave the Murphys', Bart turned to Sophie, "Your man home yet?" She gave a negative shake of her head.

Florence Murphy spoke up: "It's a strong old boat he's on. Lots of Tilghman fellas sailed on her years there weren't neither arsters."

As the camper passed the Methodist Church, I noticed that the parking lot and road were filled with cars. I asked about it and learned that it was a Tilghman tradition to have a four-hour gospel sing at the church on New Year's Eve. After the sing, things grew a little less pious. In past years a lot of the older islanders would dress in masquerade costumes after church and go visiting their neighbors. Now some still went masquerading; others just went visiting. Someone in the camper said it was a night when women waited for "second story artists"—lovers, not burglars.

The bottle of whiskey made its rounds. The camper cruised St. Michaels. One of the crewmen, Tommy, already seemed fired by the liquor; he alternated between teasing the women about their sex lives and calling challenges to cars passing on the street. Tommy's companions laughed at his antics, but ceased passing the whiskey in his direction.

At the Quarter Deck the men of the *Ruby Ford* and the three women with us joined tables filled with St. Michaels watermen, including Billy and Ginny Adams and the Marshalls. A brassy rock and roll band played as if to drive the freezing weather away from the gathering place. A fire in the central hearth helped. Dancing seemed a ritual of the winter; everyone did it with resolution. For the first time in weeks I felt hot.

Between dances, drinks and conversation flowed without much direction. Men talked log canoes. Should the class rules be purified to eliminate a lot of the modern gadgetry? Is a big or a small canoe better for racing in the Tred Avon River? Which skipper is the handiest sailor? Who is the best crew manager? Who has the best crew? Why is the jib tender the most important crew member? Would Bart Murphy tend jib for Junior Marshall on *Rover* next summer? Maybe, maybe not; depends on how good the crabbing season is for Bart. What a team though, Murphy and Marshall!

Women joined the conversation about log canoes for a while but drifted into a discussion of children. They appraised the appearance of a friend who was pregnant. They compared the way this woman carried her baby to a number of women they knew who had delivered small babies with very short labor. They told tales of abrupt and dangerous births on Tilghman. Many of the women from the island never made it to the hospital in Easton. The women decided that their pregnant friend should alert the Coast Guard that she might be needing the services of a helicopter. The chopper crew was used to the call.

In the midst of this Billy Adams proposed a toast to his wife: "For waitin' on me for twenty-six years, for workin' on the water. Happy anniversary." People cheered. They ordered rounds of drinks. Everyone passed out kisses at midnight. Tommy put his head in his hands and passed out. Someone asked Sophie if Peter was home from the water yet. She shook her head and pursed her lips. Couples began taking leave.

It was 1:00 A.M. and the *Ruby Ford*'s gang was in the camper again. The whiskey bottle made its rounds more slowly now. The truck twisted over dark roads. The propane heater died. The truck rolled on, and the men and the women in the camper pressed together for warmth.

At last the truck stopped in front of an ancient Cape Cod house in the woods.

"Where are we?" asked Tommy, waking momentarily from his sleep.

"Peter and Sophie's," said someone.

The house was almost as cold as the outdoors. We built a fire in the wood stove.

With the stove churning and the gas oven and burners flaring, the house began to thaw. Tommy was put to sleep on the couch. Country blues drifted from a tiny stereo system. For a while Bobby and his wife danced. When the record ended, the dancers joined their circle of friends leaning together on the floor in front of the wood stove. For what seemed hours, the men and women sat together barely speaking. Some sipped beer, some sipped tea. In the cottage the only light besides what filtered from the oven and wood stove was the glare of the candles on the Yule tree. Cloth shapes of skipjacks, skiffs, and ships hung from the spruce and cast moving shadows on the walls. Someone suggested we sing carols.

Long after the songs died, the front door opened and a thin, bearded man dragged in a duffle and kissed his wife. After twenty-eight days, Peter had come home.

New Year's morning the pipes were frozen in my house, so I trudged toward Gary's Phillips station for some coffee and warmth. Fog swirled over the island and crystalized on everything including my down parka and tossle cap. Breathing was like inhaling gravel. Everything sparkled grey. As I stumbled past Dogwood Cove, I bumped into one of my crew mates, Charlie Buck. The man was busy clearing ice from the bilge of a crabbing skiff with a hatchet and a butane torch. The ice in the bilges, as well as on the harbor, looked like marble.

Charlie Buck spoke when he saw me: "Wish we had the old times if this is the way it's goin' to be. Rather be warm and poor than cold and poor. They say it's goin' to rain today. Well, I'd say it's goin' to rain ice cubes, wouldn't you?"

I muttered an obscenity in agreement and headed for Gary's.

In the front storeroom old men I didn't know had stationed themselves on benches. I warmed my hands on the coffee urn and listened to the old men talk.

"When I come here twenty-five years ago, I paid $60 tax on five acres. Now I sold off all my property except a sliver and I got to pay $300."

"Man can't afford neither of it."

"Blame it on the state."

"That ain't right; they've been regular with us."

"Hell, you say."

One man told a story about how the state attempted to manage the construction of Dogwood Harbor. It touched off family squabbles. Neighboring relatives had bickered over who owned how much of the waterfront—the state was paying premium prices for what had always been valueless marshland—"Took years for some of that family to make up to each other."

"It's just like that open drainage ditch they dug along Main Street. It's a nuisance. A little kid or even a car like to get lost in that thing. I know some people that are working hard at filling that ditch with beer cans. You wait, either year now the town's goin' to decide to lay drainage pipe in the ditch and find the thing filled. Whole thing's goin' to have to be dug again; only this time some contractor'll make a fortune recycling the metal cans. Yes, sir, look how long they was at gettin' the Narrows channel drudged deeper."

"Said it was the weather that give 'em problems."

"Friggin' weather. They don't know what weather is. Them state boys might believe the ice age was on to 'em if they saw this island now."

"Weather. I'll tell you what it's done to taxes over the . . ."

Weather and taxes, taxes and weather. I drew a fourth cup of coffee and moved to the pool room in the back of the building. I wanted to blank the talk of hard times from my mind. I found a game of "nine ball." Four of us played for a quarter a ball. The crack of the balls, the smooth shaft of the cue, and the calls of "get tight, get tight" as players cheered their shots into bunched formations diverted me for almost two hours. I gave my last quarter as a tip to one of the ten-year-old boys who seemed to make a living fetching coffee and candy from the front room for the pool players. It was time to go home.

As I began putting on my coat to leave, a man dressed in a snowsuit strode into Gary's store and called to several of the men I had played billiards with. The young men circled him as he talked rapidly, "C'mon, boat's trapped in the Narrows ice and bustin' up!"

The men bought several six-packs of beer and dashed out the door. I followed them to a tonging boat that was as big as a shipjack. The snow-suited man cranked the engine of the vessel as the others boarded and passed out beers, long gaffing poles used for docking, and coils of extra line.

The big tonging boat was locked in ice. Immediately men began chipping at the ice from around the boat with their gaffing poles. At first the frenzy of the work made me wonder if I were aboard the endangered vessel, but as the boat rocked back and forth and finally broke into clear water in the center of the Narrows, the fog lifted some and I saw the outline of a small tonging skiff caught in an ice jam at the Bay end of the channel.

The bigger vessel moved deliberately toward the stranded boat, and the watermen took their first swigs of beer. They had worked up a sweat breaking their boat free of the ice at its mooring. When the big boat reached within sixty feet of the stranded boat carrying one man, the rescue vessel stopped. Between it and the stranded craft floated thick overlapping slabs of ice. Apparently the stranded craft had tried to break out of the Narrows into some nearby tonging ground that was free of ice. But the small boat had not been powerful enough to break its way clear. Before it had a chance to turn back for its mooring, cakes of ice carried by the swift current trapped the tonger from behind.

"She's leakin' like a bitch," called the man from the stranded boat. "Can you tow me out of here 'fore I go wadin'?

"Ain't the weather for wadin', Charlie," called a man on the rescue boat as he hurled a long heavy line to his trapped friend. Men secured the towline. On the big tonging boat they worked to fend off more cakes of ice that the current was sending toward them. The propeller of the big boat beat the water and both vessels moved free for several feet.

"Stop," cried the man from the small boat. "You're goin' to bust this one up."

"Can you walk off?"

"Don't trust this ice. Can't swim."

The men on the big boat took gulps of beer and talked. Then they threw a gaffing pole to the stranded man. "Make your own breathin' room" was the command.

All the men chipped at the ice. The big boat moved ahead slowly. Stopped. Men chipped again. The boats moved a little more freely. The process repeated itself. Fog grew thick. Rescuers lost sight of their tow. The towline snapped.

"Where you at, Charlie?" called the rescuers.

"In a leakin' boat, you damn fools."

"Keep your boots on; we'll find you," said one of the men from the rescue boat.

A rescuer coiled a new towline for throwing. Another man stopped the engine. Eyes searched for the stranded tonger in the failing light and fog.

"Keep chippin', Charlie."

The sound of the gaff hook picking at the ice far away seemed to come from three different directions.

"Set a light, Charlie. You're dark as a nigger in an oyster hold."

"Battery's dead," came the word from the fog. "I got more 'n two feet o' water in here."

"Damn tongers," a dredger said and shook his head. "Neither problems like this on a drudgeboat. Been times on this Bay when air was thick as butter on deck, but a man could always find his way if they hauled him to the top o' the mast."

The pleas of the man lost in the fog grew louder.

"That's it, Charlie; you talk loud enough, and long enough, we'll find you." Several rescuers laughed and tipped their beers, but they squinted intently into the fog in the direction of the trapped man's voice. The air grew colder and darker.

It took another half hour before the searchlight of the rescue boat found the voice in the fog. Finally the men rigged a towline. An hour later, when the tide turned in favor of the rescue, the rescuers pulled the stranded boat free of the ice jam. Beer was long gone. Watermen shivered. The small tonging boat sunk at its mooring. Everything was covered with rime ice.

Back at Gary's station the old men collaborated to tell a story of fog.

"Goddamn if old Captain Ben used to puff himself up with tales."

" 'Deed he did. 'Member how he was always sayin' you could blindfold him—'put me anywheres on the Bay,' he'd say—and he could tell just where he was by tasting a bucket full o' mud hauled up from the bottom?"

"Yes, Jesus, but don't you know that gang o' colored he had sailin' with him got tired of the old man showing off everytime they lay into a patch o' fog. Imagine now, every time them niggers think they're lost souls, old Cap' Ben would order a bucket o' mud hauled aboard. He'd dip a finger in, give it a good lick, then say that he know'd they was in this place or that. He'd give 'em a heading, and he always brought 'em home. Never had to lay to an anchor waitin' for the fog to lift. But Cap' Ben was prideful and he made them niggers feel common. So didn't they try to get him.

"I remember. One day when the crew figured they might get some fog they went over to Miss Lila's outhouse and dipped a bucket full from the pit. Smuggled that bucket aboard when Cap' Ben wasn't lookin'. Sure enough, after they been drudgin' for a few hours, a fog creeps in. Can't you just imagine how them niggers were frettin' 'mong themselves knowin' that any minute the Captain's goin' to taste a big load o' shit?

"By and by Cap' Ben orders up a bucket. You know him: 'Scrape up some bottom, boys. Don't worry neither bit; my tongue's workin' just fine.' Well, them niggers fake it and give Cap' Ben the bucket o' shit. By now they are just about bustin' open to keep from laughing, and Cap' Ben swipes a lick from the bucket. He tastes it good. Kinda rolls it between his lips and his tongue.

"The way I hear it he didn't do nothin' or say nothin' for a minute. Just stood there with a mouth full o' crap lookin' proud as hell. You know how he did. Then they say he looked everyone of those niggers in the eye—one at a time and real slow 'til one o' them boys ask sorta smart, 'Where we at, Captain?' Ben swallowed and said in a voice steady as you please: 'Drop the sails, boys. We're in Miss Lila's backyard.' He made them drudgers sit there for two days 'til the fog lifted; they played no more tricks in the fog after that."

Chesapeake Bay froze solid in January. Every day on Tilghman Island there were new tales of boats sunk or broken up by the action of the ice. The federal government called this cold spell the worst winter on record. Even the famous cold winter of '34 looked mild in comparison. In February of 1934 the Baltimore *Sun* carried daily stories of curtailed ferry service and Coast Guard icebreakers rescuing freighters trapped in ten inches of ice on the northern Bay. In January 1977 the ice on the northern Bay measured two feet thick, and the Chesapeake was closed to shipping north of Baltimore. Ice trapped tugs and fuel barges as far south as Virginia. Ice and tides pulled pilings out of the bottom of the Bay, twisting docks, wharves, and boat slips along the shoreline of Bay Hundred. The governor of Maryland worked to get the president to declare the Chesapeake Bay a national disaster area, making the watermen eligible for welfare and low-interest business loans. Meanwhile, many watermen struggled to repair fractured plumbing and overloaded furnaces in their homes. Other unemployed men gathered at Gary's Phillips station or the Carpenter Street Tavern.

While my money lasted I made the rounds. I helped friends with plumbing and heating repairs, loafed at Gary's station, and drank in St. Michaels. A lot of watermen began their workless days at 8:00 A.M. with coffee, beer, and conversation at Carpenter Street.

The bar in the mornings always seemed fresh. The smoky air, darkness, and dry heat from the night before were gone. The air was cool; the open curtains let the sun cast large patches of light on the drawings of traditional Bay sailing vessels that hung from the walls. In the mornings, men who had worn dirty clothes, smelled, and talked too loud the night before, were clean-dressed and shaven. They mixed whiskey with their coffee, smiled at the bright day, and talked quietly to anyone who would listen.

Billy Adams spoke to the bartender, "Those pile drivers and boatyards sure gonna have a good spring's work, ain't they?"

"This cold's got to make some work," said a man down the bar.

"Tell you what," said another. "It was so chill last night— believe the old lady and me nearly froze together for good. That's OK. If you can't eat, love."

"You got it right about not eatin'. I ain't been up to Easton [unemployment office] yet to see about applyin' for my $89 [per week], but there's lots that have. If the government's goin' to give it away, I may as well go and get it this time. Been workin' on the water and payin' taxes now twenty-seven years. Never been on the dole. This time may be different. Paid $900 unemployment compensation for my crew already this year. They may as well collect it."

"Those gunnin' party guides got it bad. They may as well put their decoys away for the season. Ice ruined the water gunnin' and I don't believe anyone wants to sit in a frozen field blind any longer. They made right smart money 'fore Christmas, though. Some carried three parties every day. Hell, those boys'll get by."

"We'll all get by. Bunch of us cut some holes out in Broad Creek. Caught five bushels of the commonest arsters I ever seen yesterday. Man paid twelve dollars a bushel. He's hard up as me."

"Yeah, good. But either time the freeze comes, it kills the market sooner, or later. When the ice goes out, price o' arsters won't be much. Way it always is."

"I hear the state's thinking 'bout extendin' the season. An extension would be OK, but it won't do lots. People stop buyin' arsters in March."

"Fella told me them Dorcester County watermen are over to Annapolis right now askin' the House of Delegates to allow unlimited power drudgin' from any boat when the ice goes out. That ain't right."

"I'm not for it, but if it's most of the others [watermen] wants it, I'll go along."

"Might have four or five good years 'fore we catch all the

arsters there is. When that happens, guess I'll have to do something else, capt'n a yacht or something. I'd rather sail for arsters than do anything. If those politicians want to kill me, well, I guess they'll have to work at it," said Bart Murphy.

"Yeah, time may be comin' when I'll have to shoot a couple of those swans in the back creek. Know it's against the law, but God put them there for a reason. I knowed it was goin' to be bad cold weather. Saved some money. Lots that didn't."

"That's me and I been gettin' drunk 'bout every day. Had some bad nights, if you know what I mean. Had some good mornings, though."

"You'll make it."

"Yeah, I might go in with some of those boys who bought old cars. They been towing drudges with them a couple miles off Poplar Island. Heard one crew got eighty or ninety bushels the other day. Way I look at it, something always turns up."

It was true. During the second week of January, Bart Murphy called his dredging crew. Murphy said the ice was more than a foot thick and he wanted to know how many of his boys were willing to risk dredging through holes in the ice. All six men were ready, so that afternoon Bart bought a 1971 Simca for $100. The next day the crew removed the doors and cut off the car's roof to make it easy to escape if the car broke through the ice. They rigged two 200-foot lines to a dredge called a "hand scrape" (smaller than the dredges towed by a skipjack) and loaded chain saws, shovels, picks, axes, and hot coffee aboard the Simca.

Early the next morning Murphy's crew strapped tire chains on their car and followed four other vehicles to an oyster bar off Poplar Island. With pick axes and chain saws they cut a line of holes in the ice at 30-foot intervals. They tied one of the lines from the hand scrape to the end of a 30-

foot pole and fed the line along from hole to hole until it stretched 200 feet. Then the holes at both ends of the 200-foot line were made large enough to drop the dredge through. With the dredge poised at the edge of one of the end holes, and the Simca tied to a towline at the other end hole, Murphy's crew was ready to catch oysters.

The captain drove the car. Three crew members positioned themselves at each end of the line of holes. One crew dropped the dredge through their hole onto the oyster bar and held the 200-foot towline that wasn't attached to the car. Then Murphy began driving the Simca away from the line of holes. He pulled the dredge across the oyster bar at less than four miles per hour. When he had driven 200 feet forward, the dredge appeared at the hole nearest the car. The crew pulled the dredge onto the ice, emptied it, and began culling the oysters. The towline was untied from the car's bumper, and Bart Murphy drove the Simca to the hole furthest from the dredge.

Murphy pulled the dredge in the opposite direction. The chill factor was thirty degrees below zero. For the first hour the dredgers were so impressed by the ingenuity of the process they didn't notice that they had lost all feeling in their faces.

As the morning passed the catch grew smaller. Culling a few oysters was not enough to keep warm. The men swung their arms in broad arches and clapped their hands together behind their backs and in front of them.

"Damn, I'm out a shape for this cold," said one of the men who skipped from one foot to the other while he swung his arms.

"Too many mornings warming yourself at Carpenter Street," said a crew mate. "Careful. Say booze thins the blood; believe it's froze right many watermen to death."

"It's a lie; I ain't come to work sober neither day this season. I ain't dead."

"You ain't worked, either. Bitchin' and cryin' that's what you been doin'."

"Says who?"

The men weren't jesting. They were glad when a new dredge load of oysters appeared: it took the crew's minds off themselves and the cold. The captain inspected the dredge's poor haul; then he ordered his crew to elongate their dredging hole by cutting it into a rectangle. The men at the other end of the operation did the same. The elongated holes opened up new bottom for dredging. The men were busy again. They began to share cigarettes.

By noon Murphy's crew had enough oysters to load the car like a coal truck. The Simca entered Tilghman on its way to the seafood buyers' with men riding atop their mound of oysters. Women and children in passing cars waved, and the old men in Gary's came outside to humor the dredgers:

"Where'd you find them arsters; just layin' on top o' the ice?"

"Them some of the scarce forest arsters you boys found?"

"Law man wouldn't be lookin' for ya, would he?"

"Ain't been power scraping on the tongers' ground, have you?"

I began to realize that dredging from a car over bottom reserved for tonging was illegal. At the buyer's the crew shoveled the oysters out of the Simca quickly. Bart handed each man eighty-four dollars for the morning's work. The money felt fresh and stiff. Legal or not, the crew had earned it, and it paid off the food bill at Miss Mary's store.

For the next ten days the crew of the *Ruby Ford* dredged with the Simca. On the eleventh day the weather warmed to above thirty-two degrees. Bart Murphy's men could feel the ice shudder as the car's chains clanked along off Poplar Island. Twice the lips of the dredging holes broke as the crew hauled the dredge onto the ice. Once the mate, Bobby, fell in the Bay up to his waist before his crewmates caught hold of his coat and fished him out. When loud cracks began sounding across the Bay, Murphy headed his crew for home; he said that the cracks were the sounds of ice working away from the shoreline. Back at the oyster buyer's, *Ruby Ford*'s crew learned that two of the other groups of dredgers had lost their cars. No one was hurt, but it had been a long walk home.

Word had it that a team from the Department of Natural Resources had been scouting around Tilghman during the day for shellfish violations. The Simca was emptied and parked in some weeds behind Bart's house; car scraping was over. It was time to find a new pastime, like Billy Adams, who had gone back to his summer job as a boatyard carpenter.

Another prediction from a jawing session at Gary's Phillips station came true: the *Ruby Ford*'s crew decided to build an iceboat.

Every morning the *Ruby Ford*'s crew gathered in a shed at the oyster buyer's to work on their "project." With drills, torches, a binful of hardware scavenged from a dredgeboat, and lumber "borrowed" from a nearby construction site, the men followed the directions of their captain. What did Bart Murphy know about iceboats? He had seen pictures. Take a mast, rig, and sail from a small catamaran; secure them to some two by eight-foot timber bolted in a crucifix; add runners to the two arms of the cross; and fix a runner on a bicycle fork to the nose of the machine for steering. It was as simple as that, said Bart.

Four days after the "project" was conceived, Murphy and his crew unloaded the icemachine, *Ruby Ford II*, from a pickup truck parked at the edge of the Miles River in St. Michaels. The struts of the iceboats spread out over the surface of the frozen river like the legs of a water spider. Murphy raised the sail and climbed aboard, sitting on the intersection of the longitudinal and transverse struts. His crew lined up behind the machine ready to push.

"Ready, Cap?"

"Ready as a goddamn astronaut. Do it," said Murphy, pulling on a motorcycle helmet.

The men leaned into the machine. It moved. They ran, pushing. Murphy guided the boat up the river perpendicular to the wind. He trimmed the sail. The next thing the crew knew they were tumbling over each other on the ice. *Ruby Ford II* clacked away from them.

The crew made for the truck. "Down the river man. Get down the river," shouted the mate. He pointed after the disappearing sail as Charlie Buck steered Bart's truck onto the ice and gave it the gas.

Watermen piled into the cargo bed and called directions.

"Follow his tracks, boy."

"Third gear, keep her in third gear."

"Watch the turn; where's the captain?"

"Here she come."

"Sail the boat, Cap. Sail the vessel."

"Give him room, boy, he got the wind."

Charlie Buck swung the truck into a 180-degree sliding turn as Murphy banged past.

"Get in his lee, give him room." The truck pursued.

"Sail the vessel, Cap'n Bart; sail the vessel, man."

"What's the speed? What's she sailin'?" yelled Murphy.

Charlie Buck held four raised fingers out the window.

"Steamin' forty, Cap. Forty! Let her rip."

"Old Bart's sailin', man. He can sail."

"Down the river boy. Down the river."

The icemachine began making wide sweeping turns in front of the truck. With each turn the windward strut of *Ruby Ford II* rose high in the air, and the skipper lay on his back along the raised strut to keep the machine from upsetting. The craft and the sailor moved in hasty gymnastics.

The ice grew rough as the *Ruby Ford II* moved out onto the broad river. Murphy reversed his craft and began clattering over waves of ice as he raced back toward the smoother surface closer to shore. Suddenly the iceboat bucked forward throwing the sailor thirty yards up the ice and flipping the iceboat on its back.

The captain was revived with whiskey. The crew towed the iceboat back to the shop for modifications; a wooden runner had shattered on the rough ice. Bart spent the rest of the day in St. Michaels pubs retelling the adventure. "Right good fun," repeated Murphy, "right good fun."

Two other Tilghman Island groups followed suit and rumors spread that some of the "down Bayers," Deale Island skipjack crews, had put together more than twelve ice-sailing rigs. Day after day, Bart and his crew worked at getting their machine "right." They tried longer wooden runners, but these too broke on rough ice. They cut runners from old pieces of railroad track, but the craft still tripped over rough spots. Finally Bart Murphy ordered a pair of forged steel runners specially built in Baltimore. With the new runners the craft sailed well.

Bart said he was practicing. The National DN Class Iceboat Races and World Gold Cup Iceboat Races were scheduled for the first week in February at the Miles River Yacht Club in St. Michaels. Murphy's crew planned to be there. Word passed around the Quarter Deck and Carpenter Street that the watermen were planning an "unlimited class" event for the iceboating fans. *Ruby Ford*'s crew challenged all comers.

The "unlimited" race never happened. Two days before the watermen had hoped to gather on the Miles River, the weather warmed enough for a small patch of water to spread over an oyster bar just off Tilghman Packing Company's seafood processing plant. On the day of the planned race, I was awakened by Bart Murphy at 7:00 A.M. and told to get dressed.

"We're goin' tonging," said Murphy. "Hurry up."

"What about the races?" I asked.

"Later. Got a boat loaned to us, and we're gonna catch some arsters while ther's some to catch. It's clear water, boy." Everyone from Tilghman and Deale Island went oystering that day.

After tonging Bart took his iceboat for a spin. He hit a soft spot in the ice. The nose runner stopped dead, Murphy was thrown clear, and *Ruby Ford II* shattered into kindling. The waterman laughed, "S'ppose it's time to go drudgin' again."

The true thaw didn't come until two weeks later, but the weather stayed warm enough for Bart Murphy and many of the other Tilghman watermen to earn money hand-tonging. The 8:00 A.M. whiskey and beer crowd thinned in the bars, and by the first week of March the *Ruby Ford* had gone back to work under sail, earning seven dollars a bushel for her crew.

Friday, March 4, seemed like a perfect day. The temperature was above fifty degrees by eight in the morning. The *Ruby Ford* worked off the Western Shore of the Bay. The wind was light and variable, but Bart Murphy kept his vessel moving. Bernard and I worked together on the starboard dredge. The men rolled up their shirt sleeves. Hours passed as we culled oysters and Bernard sang:

> I got sunshine on a cloudy day;
> When it's cold outside
> I got the month of May;
> I guess you'd say
> Nothing makes me feel this way
> Like my girl, talkin' 'bout my girl . . .

Bobby started on Bernard, "Damn, Bernard, you in love again?"

"Every spring, boy."

"You too old."

"Ain't never too old. Love's good for your head."

"And bad for your wallet."

"Can't argue that," said Bernard. "But tell me, you planning to get rich working on this drudge boat?"

"Got no plans."

"Plan on love. Make you right. Forget the drinkin' and this drudgery. Love and live."

"Be dyin' weather if you're not watchin' your black ass, Bernard."

"Why you always talking such trash, white boy?"

"Look at them clouds, Bernard," the mate pointed over the Western Shore. "Clouds like that ain't trash," he said.

The puffs of fair weather cumulus clouds that had been floating over the Western Shore a few minutes earlier had massed into a line that followed the coast. The belly of the cloud line darkened as the crew watched pillars of white vapor climb rapidly above the grey line.

"Smell the breeze, boys," called the captain.

A warm moist gust slipped over *Ruby Ford* carrying the smell of manure from the farms on shore.

"Lord, I know what's comin' next," said Bernard. "Next thing you're goin' t' hear the old wind moanin' and sighin'. Cap'n's goin' to say, 'haul them dredges, Bernard. Drop that jib, Bernard. Get sail off her, Bernard. Hold on for your black butt, Bernard!' I see it now; it's goin' be some spring squall, sure."

"And all the time you talkin' on about love like some old magpie. Them geese know what's comin' 'fore you, Bernard." Large flights of geese wheeled over the Bay.

Another of the crew noted the geese: "Seems like enough of these fellas survived the chill weather, don't it? Squalls got 'em stirred just about enough to start north."

"You best hope not. Be the end of drudgin' season," said Bart Murphy. "Look to your work, boys; ain't made up for that ice, yet."

The breeze freshened and for the next hour we worked swiftly. Several men sang to themselves.

A gust shook the jib and mainsail. The boat stood up straight, then rolled steeply on her side.

"Let go the sheets," cried the captain.

We let the sails fly free. The skipjack settled back to a less precarious angle of heel. The breeze came hot and moist.

The captain gave the commands Bernard had predicted. "We're scuddin' home. Hang on, boys," called Murphy as he steered his craft running east toward Tilghman before the storm.

Under a reefed mainsail alone the old sloop careened ahead of steep waves that would carry the boat for a few seconds on their crests, then roll under the hull and break before the bow in a rush of foam. The crew sat down on the workdeck, and held on to the winding machine.

"Damn, some fine sleigh ride," smiled Bobby. "Don't get scared now, Bernard." The mate put his arm around the black as if to comfort him.

Ruby Ford rolled and creaked.

"I'm just glad I'm with Captain Bart," said Bernard. "He's a sailorman. He knows the vessel; she's stronger 'n most. He knows the vessel good."

Bart Murphy outran the squall.

Back along the wharves large numbers of watermen counted wads of cash. Women, children, and dogs came down to the water to see the men home. A warm Friday. God, how long had it been? Little Bart and Florence Murphy lingered on *Ruby Ford* until gale winds and hailstones drove them home.

The next morning news reached the watermen of Bay Hundred that the skipjack *Claude W. Somers* from Deale Island had sunk in Hooper Strait with all hands lost. The six deaths were the first skipjack fatalities in almost ten years.

On Saturday morning at Gary's Phillips station everyone talked about the loss of the *Claude Somers*.

"Heard she got caught in one helluva local thunder squall."

"That old boat leaked pretty bad."

"Ain't what took her down."

"Fella said she'd already lost her push boat and was scuddin' 'fore the storm."

"Heard they called the Marine Police for help and the police wouldn't go."

"Is it true?"

"Don't know. They're investigatin'."

"Good luck."

"But what got her?"

"Some say she had her wheel tied in a becket [a cord to prevent the wheel from turning]."

"It's likely she got to leakin' bad and old Thompson Wallace, her skipper, put the becket on the wheel so's he could get the aircooled pump runnin'."

"I know he had one."

"Probably the crew was too scared to run the pump or take the wheel either."

"Guess she got turned sideways to the waves when the skipper was up forward, and the seas just rolled her over."

"Course nobody'll ever know."

"Happens fast as lightnin'."

"Don't take much time at all in this water till you wake up dead."

"Five of 'em was related."

"All niggers. The captain, too."

"Widows wouldn't talk to the reporters."

"Way it ought to be. It's a waterman's goddamn business and his family's."

"Not a winter that a few boys don't come home."

On Sunday, March 6, the *Sunday Sun* reported the sinking and ran an aerial photo of the wreck's rig rising above the waves:

> Hooper Island Light House, Maryland (Special)— Marine Police and Coast Guard vessels yesterday found the bodies of five men believed to have drowned late Friday when their Chesapeake Bay skipjack capsized and sank in Hooper Strait near here. The body of the sixth man was recovered Friday night.
>
> The five men were found aboard the wreckage of the boat *Claude Somers* which sank in about fifteen feet of water, Natural Resources Police reported. The sixth man was found floating in the water near the boat's wreckage.
>
> Five of the victims were related to each other, friends said.
>
> Investigators said they believed the boat was captized and overturned when struck by a heavy squall or storm sometime between 7:00 P.M. and 8:00 P.M. Friday.

89

The fifty-five-foot long vessel used for dredging oysters and clams was based at Deale Island. It was reported overdue at 5:00 P.M. Friday, police said.

At 6:40 P.M. the tug *Interstate* reported seeing the boat at anchor at Hooper Strait, which is off lower Dorchester County and separates Bloodsworth Island from the Eastern Shore.

Initial reports at that time were that the vessel was having mechanical problems. The skipjacks on the Chesapeake form the only fleet in the United States that still works under sail. The sails are raised during oyster dredging. The craft are usually equipped with motors, used for locomotion to and from the oyster beds.

At about 11:00 P.M. the body of Thomas H. James, Jr., 20, of Princess Anne was found floating in the water by other boatmen. At that time, the Coast Guard and Natural Resources Police began an active search for the boat.

The skipjack apparently sank right to the bottom with only its mast and bowsprit showing through the water.

Police boats, Coast Guard boats, private boat owners, and a Coast Guard helicopter were brought into the search. They went over most of the strait around Bloodsworth Island before finding the vessel about a mile north of the strait proper.

The wreckage was found about 12:35 A.M. yesterday, police said. They searched through the night for survivors, finding only two fuel drums and scattered parts of the craft.

Divers went into the ship yesterday morning but found that the water was too murky and muddy to see anything. About 11:00 A.M. officials began towing the sunken ship to shallower water.

By 1:00 P.M. all of the missing men's bodies had been found, police said.

Besides Mr. James, police identified the victims as Thompson Wallace, 55, of Deale Island, the boat's captain; Gerald Wallace, 24, the captain's son; Levin C.

Johnson, of Oriole, Md., an employee; George Wallace, of Salisbury, the captain's brother; and Carter Wallace, nephew to the two senior Wallaces. Mr. James was a cousin of the Wallaces, his father Thomas H. James, Sr., said last night.

The senior Mr. James said his son often went out on the bay with Captain Wallace, an independent operator.

He said that Gerald Wallace was home on a ten-day leave from the Navy and had just decided to accompany his father on the boat.

Mr. James added that normally the boat is out for four or five days at a time, but because of the still present ice danger on the water, it has been returning each night.

"As long as I've been around, Thompson Wallace has been out hunting oysters," Mr. James said, adding, "This [accidental death] is something people don't look forward to, but you know it happens."

Spring

ince the end of oystering season the state was paying dredge boats like *Ruby Ford* forty cents a bushel to catch loads of small young oysters, called spat. This spat will grow into market oysters in one to two years. Dredge boats caught spat in the Choptank River and replanted their loads on hand tonger's ground west of Tilghman. Bart Murphy had gone eeling up at the head of the Bay, but he put his mate, Bobby, in charge of dredging *Ruby Ford* through the spatting season. The skipjack was earning her captain a boat share even while Murphy was working on his own power boat, *At Last*. *Ruby Ford* gave me a living during this slack period between oystering season and crabbing season. The skipjack's crew consistently caught more than a thousand bushels of spat daily. The work paid well.

The day before Easter it stormed. The spat boats and eelers stayed in port. A lot of men gathered at the Carpenter Street Tavern. There was the usual bar talk: "Charlie gettin' any crabs yet? Seen he had a trotline set over to Broad Creek yesterday."

" 'Bout a bushel's all he caught. Too damn early for that foolishness."

And there was almost a fight between Bart Murphy and a tonger. The tonger had complained too long and too loud to Bart about the damage dredging did to the oyster beds. Bart was about to go after the tonger with a chair when Billy Adams and Junior Marshall separated them. Then there were the dart games and the poker until late into the night. I had recently taken to gambling over dart games in a number of local bars.

I overslept the next morning, waking late for a date I had made days before. I was to escort M'Ada Harrison and her two sisters to the Tilghman Methodist Church for Easter service. I ran to M'Ada's house. I was still wearing my clothes from the day before.

M'Ada stood arm-in-arm with her two sisters in front of her house. She was taller and thinner than the women at her flanks. Her white hair, white skin, and white shawl over a silver dress made me blink.

"You look like to die, boy," said M'Ada.

I blinked again.

"Never seen anyone readier for the Lord," said one of the shorter women in a crimson dress.

Another blink.

"Ready for the celebration of the blood of the lamb," said the third woman in green.

"Look sharp, you," said M'Ada. "They'll be no waterman that's spattin' on the Lord's resurrection."

I opened my mouth to apologize for my lateness and shabby appearance.

"Don't," said M'Ada. "There's half the island's men goin' to say those words this mornin'. Don't need one more. Just get cleaned up. Ethel's driving."

When I returned in a new suit from my shower and shave, the windy morning filled with the sound of bells. M'Ada Harrison offered me her arm. I escorted her to Miss Ethel's twelve-year-old blue Chevrolet.

We drove down Main Street. Knots of people in stiff clothes moved southward through the patches of sunlight toward the church. On the broad plain of the island weathered houses sat in sharp outline against the blue of the Bay and sky. Grass grew thickly on the lawns beneath a few willows, poplars and black walnuts. The air filled with the unmistakable smell of oysters and crabs that drifted off the shellpiles of Tilghman Packing Company, near the Methodist Church.

One of M'Ada's sisters turned to me. "You don't think you'll get sick?" she asked. "You sure ain't lookin' well this mornin'."

"Too bad; the Reverend's goin' to cure that," said the other.

"You mean the good doctor Jesus."

"I mean the Lord's goin' to give some comfort and unburdenin' to right many watermen," said M'Ada.

"Don't you worry about that. The Lord got the power or this island like to have sunk before our great, great, granddaddy caught an illegal oyster and drank whiskey."

"He's got to love the watermen. St. Peter was one. Wild and worthless. 'Til Jesus loved him."

"And after."

"He came to found the church."

"Was his workin' on the water, and his sinnin', brought him to the Lord."

"Seen death on the water and tasted hell in the taverns. Knew he couldn't face it all alone."

"Watermen carry that special burden. Jesus goin' to lift that weight." The car stopped in front of the graveyard.

"Glorious day," M'Ada said. "Nice to have a man to church, again."

The other women agreed.

The front seat of the car was filled with vases of carnations, gladiolas, and lilies. The women passed the flowers out to me: "Here's for the men's graves. T'other two's for the altar."

When we finished unloading the car, M'Ada Harrison handed me two vases of flowers. "From my garden," she smiled and motioned with her hand for me to follow her out into the field of headstones behind the red brick church. The old lady and her sisters tramped in single file down the rows of stones. Each carried flowers held in front of her.

I followed, stopping when the procession halted to read on a stone:

> Call not back this dear departed
> Anchored safe when storms are o'er
> Gone but not forgotten
> This tablet is erected to his
> Memory by his wife

The woman placed flowers. We bent our heads for a moment, then moved on.

There were more stones and more stops. One was before a tablet engraved with a large skipjack sailing into a sunset. The epitaph challenged: "Jesus Saves. Ye must be born again. Do you know him? He is willing. Are you?"

Around in front of the church families thronged with slow Sabbath deliberation. Most of the men looked old and wore black or flat brown. Their faces were lean and dark. They gathered in clusters on both sides of the walk mumbling words like "hefty sooks" and "red-legged jimmies"—crab lore set spinning by the spring weather. I recognized many of the men from my revelry the night before. They nodded to me with smiles of conspiracy.

M'Ada Harrison had my arm firmly locked in hers, so I had no chance of lingering with acquaintances outside the sanctuary. Instead I followed the parade of families indoors. How different the women and children looked from the men. Dressed in bright colors they showed the plump white skin of their English ancestors. The church was filled.

M'Ada Harrison directed me to place the flowers I was still carrying on the left and right edges of the altar. The choir was already in place and cooling themselves with hand-held fans.

"Praise the Lord, Brothers and Sisters!" The words came in a tenor drawl from a middle-aged man with an unmanageable cowlick. He stood at the pulpit.

"Praise the Lord, Brother," the congregation replied.

"My, isn't it a privilege to gather on such a fine day to rejoice in eternal life?"

"Amen."

"Do you believe that Christ died that ye shall live eternal life?"

"Yes, Brother."

"Do you believe that Christ died that ye may not fear to cross the water? That ye may not fear the dark cloud or the restless waves? That love and peace abideth on the other side? Oh, death, where is thy sting? Oh, Jesus, how sweet your voyage sailed." The minister spoke on. The dim room filled with an irregular hum of "Amens." Then the speaker's arms spread wide from his shoulders and rose above his head. "Brothers and Sisters, let us sing for our deliverance "Jesus Savior Pilot Me."

I rose and shared a hymnal with M'Ada Harrison.

> Jesus Savior, pilot me
> over life's tempestuous sea;
> unknown waves before me roll,
> hiding rocks and treacherous shoal.
> Chart and compass come from thee;
> Jesus Christ, pilot me.
>
> As a mother stills her child,
> Thou canst hush the ocean wild;
> boisterous waves obey Thy will
> when Thou sayest to them, "Be still!"
> Wonderous sovereign of the sea,
> Jesus Savior, pilot me.
>
> When at last I near the shore
> and the fearful breakers roar

'twixt me and the peaceful rest,
then while leaning on Thy breast,
may I hear Thee say to me,
"Fear not I will pilot thee."

As the refrain began, and called on the Lord to lead men
from peril on the sea, the minister's right hand reached over
his head as if trying to grasp the illuminated cross fixed on
the ceiling beam above the pulpit. The choir mimicked the
gesture. Immediately masculine arms began stretching above
the congregation toward the sky. The tones of the hymn
grew louder. Women's arms raised, too. When the song
ended there was gasping for breath throughout the church.

"Don't set down, ye lambs of God."

The congregation halted. Already their leader had deviated
from the program printed in the church bulletin.

"Who among you does not grieve for a lost loved one?
What least of you does not cry out for the soul of husband,
father, son, or brother? Where are they now? Tossing on the
black waters?"

"Oh, no!"

"Praise Jesus, he has carried them over Jordan and into
Canaan. They can hear us now, and they are happy. 'Be not
afraid,' they say. 'Tell the Lord Jesus Christ you have come
to know his love.' Oh, most merciful love that will drive
away all the pain of your sins. Who will testify?"

"Brother, I'm a sinner." A woman's voice came from the
center of the church. "I did not believe in Jesus. I'd seen the
water take our men with families. Watched my children
shiver and starve because the Bay gave up no harvest. How
could there be a Savior if he let this happen? I drifted away.
My life became ruled by the material comforts of my family."

"Mercy," came the grumble from one hundred voices.

The testimony continued: "Brothers and Sisters, I lost my

faith. Then came that awful storm around the first of March. The kids saw the storm stirrin' so I took them down to the Narrows to see if their Daddy's boat had got home safe. Buddy's boat weren't at neither wharf. The sky grew black by supper. Other men came ashore that evenin' tellin' of a wicked blow that scattered the fleet. Said boats was lost, sure. Said some of the drudgers tried to get protection on the Western Shore, others tried to race ahead of the storm down Hooper Strait. A few got back to Tilghman. No one had seen Buddy since afternoon. Then we heard over the radio 'bout a skipjack being lost. They weren't givin' names, said it was blowin' too hard for the rescue boats to get out. My little girl started crying. 'Why can't they save my daddy?' she kept sayin'. My little boy was cryin' too. Lord, I was scared for Buddy. And in my fears I turned back to Jesus. We knelt down in the livin' room and prayed the Lord's Prayer together, and we asked in a million ways for Jesus to spare Buddy. That long night I promised the Lord that I'd be his disciple if he let Buddy come home to us."

"Praise the Lord, Sister," said the minister.

"After midnight the call came: Buddy tore up some gear, but he got into Chesapeake Beach. The kids and I cried because we had felt the merciful love of Jesus."

"Amen, Amen . . ."

"Oh, Heavenly Father, be praised!" shouted the minister. "You have given us another sign through Sister Mary that we may believe in Thy amazing grace. Let us sing our testimony, Brothers and Sisters. 'Amazing Grace' from our hearts."

The organist plunged into the opening chords of the hymn. Hands raised toward the ceiling. The minister's voice called out the verses. The Harrison sisters wiped tears from their eyes. The song built to crescendo slowly. The sanctuary smelled of sweat.

"Come forward, sinners." The minister's voice, again.

"Come show Jesus you are ready to do his work day by day. Come kneel with me at the altar. Come join with the spirit of those loved ones who have crossed Jordan. Take ye this wine that is the blood and this bread that is the body that ye shall join in the kingdom of God."

Yet another chorus of "Amazing Grace" poured through the church, as people in two's and three's flowed forward to kneel at the altar and partake of the Sacraments. My elderly escorts swept me forward among the shuffling forms of watermen. In a rush of whispered words at the alter we were granted deliverance from the fear of death.

When it was over, the large doors at the rear opened. The Harrison sisters clung to my arms.

"Needed that!" A hard hand fell on my back. I turned to see Bart smiling with pursed lips.

"There were some debts paid this morning," I admitted.

"Goin' to have some fair weather, sure now," said one of the sisters.

"For Easter dinner at my house," said M'Ada Harrison.

"For paintin' the bottom of my skiff, Miss Ada," said Bart Murphy. "Crabs goin' to come any day now." He winked at me. "Got an extra brush."

"Go on boy. Man can't stay pure long." The women left.

During the final days of spatting in April the crew of *Ruby Ford* had taken to avoiding the cabin of the vessel. In the early sunrises of spring the work deck became the place where the crew would stretch out, make pillows of their oilskins, and sleep while the mate guided their skipjack on the hour and a half run to the spat beds. Below decks the stove remained fireless until calls for coffee sent Bernard down into the cabin to brew a "wake up" for the hands. Breakfast was a bologna and cheese sandwich just before adding oil and cranking over the winding machine.

It was on the last of those mornings of the winter/spring transition that the crew woke on deck with a start. Bernard was shaking them.

"Rise your asses, boys; I see we got trouble now."

"What's the matter, Bernard? You so tired from tomcattin' all night you ain't found the coffee yet?" asked Charlie Buck.

"You ain't seen tired yet. Look! Look what's cap'nin' this boat."

The men tried to focus on the figure at the wheel. It was not the thick form of the mate, Bobby. The helmsman was skinny and twisted. Black oilskin overalls and a red plaid shirt buttoned at the neck draped the man's bones. He leaned on the wheel from behind with both arms. The head thrust forward on the shoulders. Silver stubble covered the face.

"God," whispered one of the men. "Who's that?"

"If you're asking Bernard, I say it's the devil himself."

"Heard that old man was dyin'. What's that son of a bitch doin' runnin' our boat?" asked Charlie Buck.

"Why don't you ask him? See what that old bastard gives you."

"Give your black ass the heave ho. That's what."

" 'Deed he will. Just call me one shy nigger today. Watch me hide." Bernard pulled the brim of his sou'wester hat down over his eyes.

"Where'd that old man come from? Where's Bobby?" The crewmen pursued the conversation.

"Must o' been stowed away in the cabin. Damn, Bernard, why didn't you check below 'fore we cast off? This white man would have stayed ashore if I know'd that crazy old man was cap'n."

"Lord, I'd a jumped ship with you. They say he ain't never been all together, if you know what I mean."

"Loony: rammed the *Ida Marshall* when she wouldn't break tacks with him. Yes sir, he sunk her. 'Swim home, you chickenshits,' he told her crew."

"That ain't the half of it."

"Say he used to get his crews over to Bal'mer. Shanghai'd 'em, that's what. Drug men aboard when they was stone drunk and left port. Told 'em: 'Cull oysters or swim.' "

"Couldn't get crew no other way."

"Well, goddamn Bart, and damn the mate: they fixed us now."

As the men talked they pretended to be greasing the winding machine. The conversation confirmed what I had suspected: the man at the helm was a retired skipjack captain. He had not sailed regularly for more than fifteen years, but he occasionally appeared without warning at the helm of one or another Tilghman skipjack. It was never clear whether the old captain was pressed into service by skippers or mates who wanted a day away from dredging, or whether the ancient skipper had driven the skipjacks' proper managers from the vessels' wheels through trickery or intimidation. The men on the *Ruby Ford* never mentioned the helmsman's proper name. Behind his back they called him the "old man" or "old bastard"; to his face they addressed him as "captain" and "sir." The crew accused the old man of everything from piracy to murder. It was common belief that the old man lived in a perpetual rage brought on by endless sipping on pints of rum. No one on Tilghman wanted to cross the old man, and everyone said there was never another captain who could catch more oysters or break a young man's spirit the way the *Ruby Ford*'s present skipper could. A hot old man. Full of riddles . . .

"Heave up the goddamn canvas. You boys think you're niggers at a watermelon picnic or what? Get to them sails.

They'll be no pushin' for arsters while I'm cap'n. Get that push boat hauled out, Bobby." The old man's command sent the sails aloft and produced the mate who had been stationed in the push boat.

The crew lined the stern of *Ruby Ford* to haul the push boat out of the Bay, and their mate shrugged subtly to his friends as if to apologize for the old man's appearance. When the crew moved back to the work deck to break out the dredges the mate muttered: "He snuck up on me when we was a mile beyond the Narrows. Called me ten times the tail end of a mule. Got me into the push boat 'fore I knew whether to strike him or say a prayer. Coming a foul o' that old man has turned me inside out. Things is right queer. And he's queerest of all."

"Tend them sheets or you'll be walkin' home from here." The old man pointed to a slight shudder of cloth near the top of the sail, "She ain't right yet. Don't try and think about sailin'. Jus' pull on them sheets till I tell you to stop. Goin' to show these poor-excuse-for-watermen the right way to catch seed arsters. Damn 'em too if they don't make way." The old man raised his arm and gave the finger to six other skipjacks that were powering in circles over the spat bar.

"Heave them drudges."

"Ho."

The *Ruby Ford* cut across the bow of another skipjack. In the fifteen-knot breeze the sailboat raked oysters from the bottom in swift, graceful strokes. She seemed to move better than the boats under power. They rolled and pitched in the waves; *Ruby Ford*'s sails pulled her forward through the seas on a steady angle of heel.

"Don't that looney make her move some!" grinned Bernard as he helped to heave the starboard dredge into the Bay.

"Slack the jib sheet," called the captain. "Let them dredges out seven more feet. Shove them arsters up to the bow. This boat ain't sailin' square."

"Damn. Hear them orders. Didn't know you shipped on a slaver did you, boys?" asked Bernard.

"He's going to sink us if he don't stop drivin' this boat. Why she's older than he is, and we all seen them rotten places along her keel. Another thing—he ain't reefed her sail. Cap'n Bart would be crazy if he knew the old man was carrying every lick of rag in this breeze. Stay clear o' that mast, I tell you. She'll be coming down right soon."

"Heave."

"Ho."

The decks of *Ruby Ford* flexed as the dredges bit into the thick bed of spat oysters. Sometimes the dredges would load within seconds, and the weight of the loaded scrapes would make the skipjack shudder and almost stop. It was always this precise moment, when the bow of the boat seemed to trip on something and threaten to pitch down into the seas, that the old captain signaled his crew to haul their dredges. Each time the dredges dug into the bottom and the vessel began to shudder the crew wondered whether the captain would be quick enough to haul the dredges before the strain of the mast or rigging was too much. They thought about the cracks in the mast and the rot along the keel.

"Heave."

"Ho."

Hundreds of pounds of spat crashed aboard *Ruby Ford* each minute. The men took off their heavy clothes, rolled up their shirt sleeves, and started to sweat as they shoveled the spat into huge piles that began to cover the deck of the skipjack from bowsprit to wheel. The speed of the operation and the heat of the day caused the crew to ignore the wondering stares of other crews and the mutterings of their queer captain. The rhythm of the labor made them chatter thoughtlessly.

"Thought the old man's liver'd given out on him."

"That's what I'd heard, too. Bart told me they took the old man up to Easton for a week."

"Hospital?"

"To dry him out. Had the DT's. Found the captain locked in the bathroom one day—screamin' his heart out."

"God, he's a devil."

"Doctors sent him home. Said he was a goner; liver was played out."

"Now he's pirated this here drudgeboat!"

"Shows just what the doctors know, don't it?"

"Ain't one of them can figure that old man."

"Ain't me either."

"He's just balls. That's the end on it. More juice than them prize bulls they got up the road."

"Juice, you say. 'Bay Rum' I call it. Look there."

The crew eyed their master. He leaned on the wheel even more noticeably than he had when they had first seen him. His face thrust forward as if straining to call to his crew. At regular intervals he freed an arm from the wheel and reached inside his coveralls. He tossed an open pint of liquor to his lips. The shirtsleeves wiped the mouth clean.

"Heave, you monkeys," came the captain's call. "Break your backs to it or be damned."

"He's warmin' up now, ain't he?" said Bernard.

"Hot as a firecracker."

"Break his own back," called the mate before he had checked the shout. Then in a lower tone, "I ain't sweat so much in ten years."

The old man's eyes flashed at the mate, "I'll clear the world of you, donkey." With sudden speed and grace the captain rushed forward over the piles of oysters. As he moved over the piles, his hands clawed up spat, which he showered on the mate. Bobby covered his head with his arms and tried to drop behind the winding machine out of the captain's view. But the old man scrambled toward the work deck with such haste that the pock, pock, pock of the spat against the mate's oilskins sent Bobby retreating behind the oysters piled in the bow of the boat.

"One more word, jackass, and I'll drive you off the bow." The captain spun around to face the rest of the crew: "Damned if I won't. Who's goin' to make it different? Heave them drudges and mind your friend's tongue. We're not loaded yet. I want 1,000 bushels. Hear?" The captain moved back to the wheel.

The crew returned to the rhythm of haul, heave, shovel, shovel, shovel . . . The men wondered silently how the old man planned to make their skipjack carry 1,000 bushels: she was built to hold 750.

Morning passed in the swinging of shovels and the haze of sweat-soaked eyes. After an hour *Ruby Ford* began to move more sluggishly. Water came closer to her decks. Oysters covered her entire length five or six feet deep. She looked like a sailing rock pile.

A boat from the Department of Natural Resources came alongside the skipjack, "Cap'n, sir, looks like you got more'n she can carry already."

"Mind your own business," called the old man. "When I want you to tally up, I'll holler."

"I got a slip here for you; says you got 750 bushels," called the skipper of the state boat.

"Go away!" yelled the captain.

"I ain't goin' to let you sink those boys, Cap. May as well haul your drudges 'cause I am payin' for 750. That's it."

"Screw."

"That's all," said the official. "Take the ticket, Bobby." The mate reached out and took the receipt from the man on the powerboat steaming to windward of the skipjack.

"Goddamned government bastards," screamed the old captain. He spun *Ruby Ford*'s wheel. The skipjack crashed against the powerboat as that vessel veered to pull away.

"Just go plant that spat, Cap'n. Got no time for your foolishness."

The old man made a deep rasping sound as he cleared his throat and spat at the stern of the powerboat. He froze for seconds in the act of projecting the spit.

The crew watched their captain. At last he seemed to recover from a daydream. "Sheet out them sails," he said. "We got some plantin' to do."

It was a blue steel day and an hour's sail to the planting bar. The crew lay back on the spat and rested. Small seabirds, called shearwaters, hovered over *Ruby Ford*. The captain steered in silence and drank.

The crew's sleep was disturbed by the slurred words of the old man: "Shove 'em overboard. Get the blasted things out of my sight. Spat oysters—fool's gold. Wasted my life. Shove 'em quick. Got to go home."

"Drunk as a coot," muttered Bernard. "Let's get it over with 'fore he gets any worse."

They were on the planting bar. The six crewmen swung their shovels and the spat settled into the Bay. The captain left the *Ruby Ford* to steer herself. He slouched over the rail and gazed at the swirling, sinking spat. He seemed to watch his shadow gliding among those rings. By degrees the boat emptied and the scowl dropped from the old man's face.

"Hey, boy, come aft here!" The captain pointed to Bobby. "You, boy, come!"

Bobby threw a questioning look at Bernard.

"Don't ask me: can't explain 'bout that old man."

Bernard slapped Bobby on the butt, "Don't say nothin' but 'yes, sir.'"

"Come boy." The man's speech was thick; he waved his arms wildly in the air.

Bobby crawled over the heaped spat to the stern.

"Take the wheel. Sail her. Don't care where. Just unload her quick and get me home."

Bobby wasn't at all sure where the boundaries of the planting bar were, so he brought the *Ruby Ford* about and began resailing the path along which they had just planted spat. It was a route he could follow until the decks were clear.

"Steady, boy, bottom's goin' to fall out o' this breeze directly. It's comin' to a mild wind and a deep blue sky. Sixty years ago. Day like this I sailed my daddy's drudgeboat. Caught my first arsters, planted my first spat. Sixty years of chill and hazard and storms. Years of loneliness at the wheel. Called a bastard and demon. Why? Why forsake the meadowlands and a woman—left to grow old and die before her time while I was not noticin'?"

The old man sipped steadily from his pint of rum. Bobby tacked *Ruby Ford*. The crew rushed to unload the boat. The breeze was dying.

"Sick with the thought of water, boy. Sick with the torment of the sail and the catch. Feel bent and breathless with a million bushels of arsters on my back. Lord, what is that thing that kept crowding me away from the hay fields? Always the catch. The catch is the thing. Where's the peace in it? A mild breeze and a blue sky? That's the pay and that's the bait! Is it enough for you? Is it enough for any man?"

The old man took a gulp of rum and flung the bottle into the waves. "Sick and drunk," he muttered. "Take me home." The captain disappeared into the cabin below.

When the last spat sunk in the Bay, the crew rigged the

push boat and furled the sails. The old man curled like a dog on the cabin floor and dozed. No one tried to explain the events of the day. Dredging was over until the fall.

Crabs were scarce in May. In the Miles River watermen were catching four bushels a week. Broad Creek crabbers bragged about a bushel a day, and on the flats off Black Walnut Point men tallied their catch in numbers of crabs. On a good day a Tilghman Islander might land thirty legal crabs. Word circulated: the winter freeze killed most of the blue crabs. Television newsmen, seafood buyers, and environmentalists began their familiar chant: the Chesapeake was dead.

Bart Murphy didn't know about that. He had discovered new bounty in the Bay—"snakes." "Snakes" is what watermen call eels, and I joined Bart Murphy and a man called Big Henry on Bart's thirty-five-foot Bay-built workboat harvesting a half ton of eels a day.

Eels are scavengers. One of their favorite food is fish roe—any kind of fish roe. Each spring rockfish, shad, and other Bay fish spawn in the creeks at the northern end of the Chesapeake. Eels follow the spawn. *At Last* followed the eels.

Days began at four in the morning. *At Last* was moored in Worton Creek, a two-hour drive up the Bay from Tilghman Island. Murphy and his crew made the trip every day and were on the water by 6:30 A.M. It was worth the trouble. *At Last* grossed $500 a day. Even with an investment of 350 eel pots (at $6.50 a piece), holding tanks, line, and bait—even with $1,000 worth of gear lost in one spring gale—eeling was good business. Bart salted small eels and stored them in old oil drums. The salt eels sold for forty cents a pound as crab bait. The waterman sold his large eels live for fifty-five cents a pound to an operation in Rockhall, Maryland, called Eels on Wheels. Here the body temperature of the eels is decreased in slowly chilling water until the fish enter a state of suspended animation. In this state the eels are packed in ice and flown to Holland, France, England, and West Germany where they are revived and sold for over $5.00 a pound. West Germany, the largest market, imports over 5,000 metric tons of live eels each year. Ninety percent of the German-bought eels are sold to gourmets as smoked delicacies.

Big Henry, a forty-year-old construction worker turned waterman, grumbled at least four times a day, "Snakin's some slippery business." It was also slimy, smelly, and a strain on muscles. But Bart had a standard answer for all complaints: "Only crabbin's free and easy—if you can find 'em. Anyway that's summer work. Eels is proper spring business. Something sexy about it."

Sex and eels mixed strongly on a day in early June. The eels had moved down the Bay. *At Last*'s crew had been setting its gear on the edge of shoals just east of Tilghman. Now the men woke to a red sunrise. I could smell honeysuckle in the morning haze. Fermenting salt eels in drums on *At Last* added to the air a smell that reminded me of breeding pens on a Pennsylvania farm. Bushels of bait, broken up horseshoe crabs full of roe, oozed across the deck.

"Smell that snake oil." *At Last* rocked as Big Henry's 6'2", 240-pound body settled onto the boat.

"Look out, here come the snake man. He walks, he talks, he crawls for the ladies like a reptile." Big Henry danced around the workboat like Little Egypt.

"Here come one bald-headed, over-sexed waterman, you mean," said Bart.

"Here comes the Tilghman Terror," said Henry. "Ain't it right, boy?" He poked me near the groin.

"You're all talk, Henry," said Bart. "Cast off the lines. Let's see if you can catch either eels today."

At Last's engine revved in neutral a moment to clear the carbon out of the chambers, then the engine dropped into a low grumble and pushed the workboat out through the cork-screw exit from Dogwood Cove. Big Henry shifted bushels of bait to the starboard rail of *At Last*. I started an aircooled pump to keep water flowing through the eel tank that sat in the middle of the workboat like a freezer-sized aquarium. Bart steered from a wheel mounted on the aft starboard side of the boat. The sun's light catching on the wake marked off the vessel's progress with a red trail across Broad Creek.

" 'Bout time to go to Bal'mer ain't it, Big Henry?" said Bart. "Believe we might drink some beer. Then—who knows? Been some springs we been to Bal'mer and not come home 'til we was broke or throwed out of all them strip places. Henry, you get carried away some, don't you? 'Course I never do."

Bart smiled at me in a way that made me know that the trip to Baltimore was something more than a "run up the road." He smelled the eels and he was ready.

At Last churned into the morning at twenty-five miles per hour. When the boat reached a line of florescent red floats off Black Walnut Point, Bart reversed the engine and let *At Last* skid up beside the first buoy in the line. The crew pulled cotton gardening gloves over their hands. I stood along the starboard rail and snagged the buoy with a gaff hook. The buoy was attached by forty feet of warp to the eel pot on the bottom. With a fast, hand-over-hand motion I pulled the warp out of the water. The boat's bow into the tidal current made the pulling easy. After ten seconds the eel pot surfaced. It was a three-foot long wire mesh cylinder, about twelve inches in diameter, and one end of it was filled with squirming green eels.

I handed the pot to Henry who was standing just forward of me. He shook the pot over a long wooden culling box straddling the holding tank. More than half a dozen eels, some of them one and a half feet long, slipped out of the pot into the culling box. They banged and wiggled around in the box and set Big Henry talking: "Blasted sea serpents. Crawl for your lives, fishrapers." He shouted into the culling box. "Look at 'em slither. Big Henry's got to find that big hole. Little varmints fall right out. Don't like it. None of 'em. Ugly bastards."

Henry was watching the way the large eels thrashed around in the culling box until they slithered through a hole that dropped them into the holding tank. These eels died in the drum and were salted down.

"Look at 'em fill that drum there," said Big Henry as he cleaned old bait from the pot and restuffed it with horseshoe crab parts. "Better go to Bal'mer tonight. Fetch more drums. Fill this last one today, certain. Believe we on a mess o' snakes."

Henry threw the rebaited, empty pot overboard. *At Last* moved on to the next buoy.

Each pot in the first line of twenty was as full as the first one had been. Bart said that if most of the pots fished as well as this first string, the crew would make $600 for the day; new drums were essential before another day of eeling. Bart had a friend with a friend who worked for a construction company that had a lot of fifty-five-gallon drums. The trip to Baltimore was securely legitimized.

During the next three hours I pulled and Big Henry emptied and baited 250 pots. Most of the pots crawled with big, market eels. The bounty of the catch made me hardly notice the growing stiffness in my shoulders, tricep muscles, and fingers. The oily film of the eel and bait slime soaked in my gloves and took on a natural feeling. I almost forgot to take my gloves off before eating my sandwich during the 10:00 A.M. break.

Big Henry made the time pass with his litany: "Believe if old Martin would have had one of these daddy snakes he wouldn't be in jail now. See, I know his old lady: if Martin had given her what she wanted, they'd never had all that trouble. It's springtime and she just wanted some love from Martin. Way I hear it, he just ain't good at that sort of thing. Well, they got to drinkin'. You know how one thing leads to another. She say 'frog' and Martin can't jump. So here she is all hot and frustrated and feelin' like a fool. Calls Martin 'a damn capon' or some such thing. Martin's got to feel about as small as a sand shrimp. Now, he ain't just right anyway: recall he got into trouble for throwing stones at the little girls over to the elementary school—and so 'damn her' he says and sets fire to the friggin' house. Boy's goin' to be in jail for a right good time. I couldn't stand that; they'd have to shoot me first, but Martin don't seem to mind it much. The way I see it, Martin could be as free as the breeze right now if he'd taken one of these big snakes over to the old lady's and let it . . ."

"Damn, Henry. You're one crude old man," said Bart shaking his head. "Talk like that's like to get me in trouble tonight."

"It's these 'snakes' done it to me. I'm a right tidy fellow when I'm after crabs or when I'm in construction. These serpents jazz a man up. You feel it, too. Otherwise we'd find drums around here, 'stead of goin' to Bal'mer."

Bart laughed, "Could be, Henry, but we better move these last hundred pots over to that eastern ledge. They ain't fishin' much here."

The men were silent again and turned to hauling pots and stacking them in tall pyramids in the stern of the boat. The late morning grew hot. With every empty trap that came aboard, I felt the stiffness in my body more. I counted the pots—twenty, forty, sixty, eighty.

One hundred. *At Last* gathered speed and stormed along the edge of a shoal. The captain watched his depth sounder. It told him when he was exactly along the lip of the shallows and when the bottom shifted from sand to the mud that eels seem to like.

"Heave 'em fast," called Bart. "Let's get Big Henry to Bal'mer 'fore he attacks one of those goats he's got in the backyard."

At noon we emptied the live eels into a holding stage and drove to the Skipjack Restaurant in Tilghman for cold beer. Two hours later Big Henry and Bart left their wives and families on Tilghman Island and headed for Baltimore in Bart's pickup.

The first stop was the Carpenter Street Pub. As the men entered the barroom the proprietor raised his head from rinsing glasses and began pointing at Big Henry: "Out. Get out, Henry. Don't have either time for your foolishness."

"But Jake I was . . ."

"Drunk as the bride's father. Out."

"But I was on hard times and now . . ."

"You're leavin' ain't you, Henry, 'fore I call the cops?" The barkeeper moved to the telephone.

"Damn, Jake, look at me. I'm sober and respectable."

The patrons began to plead Big Henry's case: "Have a heart, Jake. Hell, I seen Henry wear that suit to church on Mother's Day. He ain't likely to get tore up in that. What'd he wear to church?"

"When's he goin' to church 'til next Christmas?" asked the bartender.

"Father's Day's comin'," prompted Big Henry. "Kids would never let me miss that."

"Give the poor guy a beer, Jake. He ain't goin' to mess his pants again."

"Not his pants I'm worryin' about; it's that tidal flood he deposits on the floor. Leaves it for me to clean up."

"Best behavior, Jake." Big Henry gave the Boy Scout signal. "Just give me a couple of beers for the road."

"Who's drivin'?"

"Bart."

"OK. Don't want you to lose your license again, Henry, for drivin' under the influence."

"I'm as straight as the judge."

"Don't kid me. The whole mess of you boys is up to no good." The bartender turned and winked at some of the other patrons as he served the beers. "Look at those sharp clothes. They don't mean church; they mean Bal'mer."

The teasing began, "What'd you tell your wife, Bart?"

"Say you goin' to a prayer meetin', Henry?"

Bart let a grin spread over his lips: "Goin' to fetch oil drums for eels, that's all. Any of you hen-pecked roosters want to come along, why, do it."

No takers.

"We got to take care of business. Come on Henry."

Bart finished his beer.

The eelers started out the door.

"Don't get lost," somebody jibed.

"I do it all for the eels," said Big Henry, going into his Little Egypt routine. He nearly fell down the front steps.

The next morning I found Big Henry and Bart sleeping on *At Last*. Neither man had been home. I asked about the trip to Baltimore.

Bart muttered: "Goddamn eels 'bout run us crazy last night. Ain't seen so many skag women in a year. Goin' to make stayin' home seem sweet."

" 'Deed it will," said Big Henry.

Bart and Big Henry pulled on oilskin overalls. I loaded eight new eel drums aboard *At Last*. We were on the Bay catching eels by 8:00 A.M.

Eels continued to be plentiful. A week after the trip to Baltimore ten oil drums filled with salt eels waited in Bart Murphy's backyard for buyers. No one bought. No one needed crab bait. The hordes of blue crabs had still not appeared in the Chesapeake. Murphy's family and neighbors began to complain about the smell of rotting eels. The waterman said not to worry: crabs would come any day now. The bait would sell.

It didn't, and *At Last*'s crew caught fewer and fewer big market eels off Tilghman. The eelers' income dropped to less than $150 per man per week. Big Henry and Bart decided to move all the pots—which they owned jointly—to the Miles River. *At Last* began to work out of St. Michaels. Eels were smaller than ever. After more than a week of working on the Miles River, driving twenty-five miles each day back and forth between Tilghman and the boat, lugging barrels of salt eels around, and chopping up masses of horseshoe crabs for bait, a new man in the crew, Dougie Spurry, had not been paid any money. Big Henry kept saying "Wait 'till we sell a mess of market eels." Bart slipped Doug fifty dollars one rainy morning when they were alone outside on the workdeck, and Big Henry found reasons to be in the cabin.

Finally the holding stage was filled with market eels, and Bart and Henry called in a buyer. Several thousand pounds of eels were sold, and the crew of *At Last* marched up the street from the landing to the Carpenter Street Tavern. Bart began to buy rounds of drinks for the bar, Big Henry started spinning words, and Dougie and I waited to see what his share of the profits would be.

"Right poor spring, ain't it?" Big Henry directed his conversation to a couple of crabbers down the bar.

" 'Deed it is."

"Heard you're gettin' forty dollars for a common bushel. Don't have to catch many to get by at that price."

"Not that many for catchin'." "We ain't been doin' much either: can't sell all them small eels no how." Big Henry turned to Bart: "I might as well retire from this business—little as we're makin'. Ain't it so?"

Bart raised his eyebrows and gave his partner a suspicious look: "Whatever you say, Henry. You're the 'snake man.' I don't know neither thing about this business. I just supply the boat, the truck, the gasoline, and half the eel pots. Listen here," Bart talked to all the men at the bar. "If Big Henry says we ain't been doin' much, if Big Henry says he's too damn poor to pay Dougie for a week's work, then it must be so." Bart's speech grew louder. He ordered another round of drinks for the bar.

Big Henry made his jolliest face, "Damn, Bart, this snakin' turned your sour?"

"Ain't the snakes, Henry. It's you."

"What'd I do?"

"It's what you ain't done. You ain't paid for gasoline for a month, you ain't helped paint the boat when we got her on the railway, and you're about to try cheatin' Dougie out of his share of the eels we sold today."

"I'm a poor man."

"You're a son of a bitchin' fat, cheap, lazy snake's what you are. Prove you ain't. Here's Dougie's share of my money; match it." Bart slapped four hundred-dollar bills onto the bar. It was twice the total amount Dougie felt he had coming.

"He didn't earn that much."

"I say he did. Match it, fat snake."

Dougie didn't want the two men to quarrel, but when he began to shake his head in agreement with Big Henry and reached out to push $300 back toward Bart, a crabber beside Dougie at the bar grabbed the young man's hand in a way that said, "Let it be: this feud has to run its course."

"Up yours, Bart. I ain't goin' to be bullied by no skinny runt." Henry spat the words with vigor, but Big Henry's words were met just as quickly by a jab to the head from Bart. Big Henry's baseball cap spun to the floor as he recoiled from Bart's punches and fell off the stool. He sat up blinking on the floor. Bart was gone. The $400 still sat on the bar. Big Henry picked up his hat. He put a fifty-dollar bill in front of Dougie and left.

"Those eeler's mean bitches," said one of the crabbers.

"Bart licked him, though, didn't he?"

"Sucker punchin'—ain't nothin'."

"Didn't ever see you stand up to Bart."

"You sayin' I can't?"

"Sayin' you ain't."

"You sayin' I'm a sissy boy?"

"What do you think?"

"Think you talk like . . ."

Dougie picked up the $450 and left the bar.

Bart's pickup didn't return to Tilghman that night, and he didn't show up at the boat to go eeling the next day. When I called Bart's house in the afternoon his wife, Florence, said Bart still wasn't home. She knew about the fight with Big Henry—rumors had sifted back through the general store. Florence told me to look in all of the bars up the road. She said Bart got in moods like this when he wasn't earning much money. There were other problems on Bart's mind, too: his father was sick, and his oldest daughter had run off to Florida with a boy. Florence Murphy was worried.

Dougie and I made the rounds of the bars. At each stop we heard the same story: Bart had been there; he had set up the bar; he drank shots of vodka; he was drunk as a coot. Try the boat; someone said he had seen *At Last* swinging to a drag anchor off the Yacht Club.

Bart's pickup sat with the door open in front of *At Last*'s slip at the town dock. The slip was empty. Dougie and I found Billy Adams working in the boatyard. We took *Yankie* and headed up Long Haul Creek toward the Yacht Club. *At Last* was anchored in the south branch of the creek, Bart lay on the cabin roof.

Yankie came along side Bart's boat, and the waterman raised himself on his elbow and gave a grin: "Ain't she a perty day, boys? Don't the water just shine like diamonds?"

"Come on, Bart. Time to go home. Family needs you."

The waterman ignored Billy Adams.

"Billy, I'll tell you what I been thinkin'. I been thinkin' old Bart's a done waterman."

"Bart, you had anything to eat?"

"Don't want nothin'. I'm a done waterman. Finished."

"Let's go up the Quarter Deck and have a steak." Dougie climbed aboard *At Last* and started the engine.

"Won't have either of it. Like to catch me some crabs, but I can't find 'em. I'm just a done waterman. That's all there is. Did you know they're goin' to take my leg off tomorrow?"

"What are you babbling about?" drawled Billy.

Bart sat up and raised his right pant leg. A bright red streak started at the bottom of the white calf, climbed up the leg, and disappeared under the knee. Blood poisoning.

"Takin' it off tomorrow. Tick did it. Lousy little tick. What the hell. Take it off. I don't care. I can't make money on the water any more."

"Who you kiddin', Bart," Billy continued. "You're makin' more money than anyone."

"Few hundred dollars a week ain't nothin'. Got to make more than that. It's right the middle of June—summertime—and I ain't caught neither crab. Hell with Big Henry and his goddamned eels. That's spring. 'Deed it's true: Bart Murphy's a done waterman. Take off the leg; I don't need a bit of it . . ."

Bart continued to rave. Billy nodded his head to Dougie and me—best get Bart home.

When the
Wind Blows
Sou'west

arrying the buzz of a thousand locusts, a southwest breeze crept over the land. White pods of sea nettles began to appear in Bay Hundred waters. Crabs had "come on." Bay temperature was eighty degrees. Day after day the air warmed to ninety-five degrees and filled with haze. July Fourth was just a week off. The price of crabs was thirty dollars a bushel. Bart Murphy was like new. Rest and antibiotics had saved his leg.

Even part-time watermen worked twelve-hour days— "Got to catch those old crabs 'fore the packers cut their prices; no tellin' what will happen after the Fourth." Bart had been "on a mess o' jumbos" for more than a week. He had made more than $2,000; he had stayed out of the bars; and he invited me to cull crabs for him—"too many for one man to handle."

The first morning I was to join Bart catching crabs on a trotline a cold front passed over Tilghman Island. The weather turned rotten. I woke at 4:30 to hear trees tearing against the side of my house. I tuned in the National Weather Service broadcast—wind velocity in excess of twenty-five knots, small craft warnings in effect. I was sure Bart would stay in port, but I called the crabber's house to be certain. Florence Murphy answered: Bart had already left for the boat. I had better hurry. Take some oilskins.

When I reached the harbor *At Last*'s engine beat loudly; Bart leaned on the starboard rail of the boat. He wore a set of black oilskins. When he saw me the crabber dumped a full cup of coffee overboard.

"Damn, boy, let's get movin'. This weather's goin' to get worse 'fore it moderates." Murphy threw the engine in gear.

As *At Last* droned out of Dogwood Cove, I noted that very few other boats had left the dock. I buttoned my foul weather jacket around my neck. There was a steady drizzle, and the boat was steaming into three-foot waves that threw sheets of spray into the work area. The morning was black. Lights on shore disappeared. The gleam of navigation beacons became occasional smears in the rain and spray. Murphy opened the throttle. Exhaust roar drowned my attempt to make small talk. The boat plunged on, not turning left or right for forty-five minutes.

Suddenly Murphy cut the power. A grey light had just begun to spread across the water. I could barely make out the silhouette of Black Walnut Point lying to the west.

"This is it, boy. This is my lay," said Murphy. He pointed to an imaginary line on the water.

I gave Bart a look that said, "I don't understand."

The drifting boat pitched sharply as a four-foot roller struck her side. We both grabbed for the rail. I fell to my knees.

"Back there," Murphy stretched his arm out toward Black Walnut Point, "is an entrance to a creek. Now, see that tallest tree on the horizon? Keep the mouth of that creek right in front of the tree. You're on the southwest edge of the sandbar. It's good crabs here. Been workin' this edge eighteen years. My lay. Set my line east from here. Keep the creek and tree lined up, I'll be right on the edge of that bar. If my depth sounder were workin' I'd show you. Twelve-foot sand edge right here."

Another wave smacked *At Last*. I was ready for this one. I only dropped on one knee.

"C'mon now, let's get the trotline overboard." Murphy threw an old piece of engine flywheel over the side of the boat. The flywheel was tied to a line.

Bart took the boat's wheel, added power, and headed east with the creek and tree in line astern. "Let the line feed out through your hand," the crabber called to me.

I braced myself in the stern of the boat and guided the line being pulled from a wooden barrel in the back of *At Last*.

"Now, throw the buoy," called the captain. The line was beginning to tug on a plastic float in the barrel. I helped it overboard. More line ran out, then a short length of chain, then line spliced with chunks of salt eels.

This was the trotline.

County law forbids crab potting in any waters except the open Bay. For Tilghman waterman like Bart Murphy who crabbed the "edges" of the Choptank River and its tributaries, the county law limits the watermen to stalking the blue crab with a trotline—a device invented well over one hundred years ago. The trotline is an adaptation of the "longline" used by New England schoonermen fishing for cod on the Grand Banks. The line is usually 3/16″ manila and 2000-4000′ long. Every 4-5′ of the line has a "snood," a separate piece of thin line to which bait is tied.

The 2,500′ of Murphy's trotline snapped over the open palm of my hand and fell into the water. Bits of bait splattered the jacket of my oilskins. Within five minutes all of the baited line had pulled from the barrel. A length of chain, buoy line, float, and a homemade anchor went overboard to mark the eastern end of the line. Murphy turned the boat around. *At Last* took a wave over the bow that made the engine cough. In spite of my oilskins, I was soaked.

"You ain't no sissy baby are you?" called the captain.

I spit salt water into the bottom of the boat with as much defiance as I could muster.

"We're goin' to make some money if you can stand this sea. Them other boys can't take it I guess. Look." The captain pointed to a half dozen crabbing boats steaming for Tilghman.

"Damn sissy babies," I said trying to copy Bart's bravado. Another sea hit *At Last* and sprawled me spread eagled over the engine box.

"Damn sissy babies," Murphy mocked at me.

Bart clapped a wooden arm over the starboard washboard of the boat. The arm extended two feet over the water. Chocks and a roller composed the end of the arm. Murphy dipped a boat hook over the side as *At Last* drifted to windward of the marker buoy. He came up with the trotline and slipped it between the chocks and over the roller. The first run of the line was about to begin.

The crabber held a dip net with a wire basket in his right hand. He steered with his left. *At Last* began to retrace her path along the "Southwest Edge." Between lurches of the boat I arranged a large rectangular "catch box" just behind the engine. Around the catch box I placed four bushel baskets. This was done according to Murphy's directions. After Murphy dipped crabs off the line into the catch box, I separated the crabs into different bushels according to their size, gender, and hardness. I had a pair of steel tongs for my work.

Murphy began to stab the water with his dip net. One, two, three, four lunges. He was not simply dipping his net in the water. Some of the crabber's lunges threw his face right down to the washboard. Once *At Last* rolled hard to starboard as the crabber lunged out. Bart's feet lifted off the bottom of the boat. His body teetered on the gunwale. But his left arm held firmly to the steering wheel until the boat rolled in the opposite direction and brought Murphy securely back aboard. He had four crabs in his net.

"Ain't moderated neither bit," the crabber said taking off his oilskins. "I'm like to go swimmin' if this surf keeps up, so are you. Best get out of these skins 'fore they drag us under."

Murphy squinted into the water. He saw the telltale signs

of a crab clinging to a baited snood nearing the surface. Turbulent waves made the crab drop off the line. The crabber dipped deep, landed a "whale."

I began culling. It was easy to separate the females; I could tell the "sooks" by their red-tipped claws and their broad belly apron. But separating the males, "jimmies," was not as easy. I segregated a dozen jumbo crabs, whose shells must have measured more than seven inches tip-to-tip, into one bushel. Then I began putting slightly smaller jimmies into a separate basket.

"You cull the 'whities'?" asked Murphy without looking.

"Sure," I said, but I had no idea what "whities" were.

A chain clanked over the roller. *At Last* had reached the end of the trotline. Murphy pulled the line from the roller and skipped aft to make it fast on a cleat in the stern. I dove to move out of the crabber's way. The bushel of medium crabs spilled. Murphy paid no attention. He gripped the line as if he were in a tug of war. The boat's engine sped up slightly. The boat pulled the line taut and a few yards to windward before the crabber cast it overboard.

"Seas made the line too slack; got to straighten her out. Runnin' a right line is all in how much slack you got. Don't want it so tight the crab feels yanked to the surface. Don't want it so slack you drag 'em and bounce 'em off on the bottom."

For the first time Murphy noticed me trying to retrieve the spilled jimmies. I had already returned a number to the bushel, but at least a dozen were still at large. Several disappeared through holes in the floorboards. Others backed into corners waving their claws and snapping their pincers. The roll of the boat spilled the crabs back into center deck. I plunged at them with my tongs. Murphy frowned.

He pulled the tongs out of my hand and threw them on the engine box. Then the crabber dropped on his knees. He waved his hands over the floor boards. Within seconds Murphy had a pile of thrashing crabs stuffed between his palms. He shook the pile over the catch box. Many of the crabs fell from Murphy's hands but several clung to his skin with their claws. I had been nipped by crabs before; I thought of Bart's pain.

"Don't hurt neither bit," said Murphy pursing his lips and banging the clinging crabs against the catch box until they let go.

"Steer the boat. You ain't culled these crabs the way I like 'em." The crabber picked up the tongs and began resorting the jimmies. "Keep these whities separate, I told you. See how 'neath their shell is still kind of soft and hollow. They ain't filled up with meat yet. Just shed. Got to sell 'em for pickin'. Won't make much for hard restaurant crabs. And you cull out these jimmies that's smaller than five inches. Can't sell them legally. Take 'em home or something. Rest of those jimmies you can mix up. That's how I've always done it, and my buyer says he's never seen prettier crabs. Man has never culled neither one of my bushels."

Bart Murphy steered the boat back to the end of the trotline. The first run had taken thirty minutes. Murphy caught twenty-eight crabs. The process was repeated. The boat rolled more than ever. On the second run the cabin door popped open and hit the bulkhead so hard that the window broke.

A fan belt broke on the fourth run and it took Bart and me half an hour to get the engine rerigged. At the end of that run the crabber reculled my bushels.

Bart stopped talking to me. All he did was plunge, plunge, plunge for the crabs; pick over my culls; and mutter about the weather—"blowin' a damn gale." He had four select bushels by the twelfth run when the trotline snapped.

We spent an hour tugging the broken ends of the line

aboard. By then it was 11:00 A.M. The sky still looked grey as dawn. My skin was white and wrinkled.

"Let's go home 'fore we lose what we made," said the captain. "I ain't sayin' you're a Jonah, boy, but I'll tell you we had some bad luck this mornin'. Two men got to catch more crabs than this. Better do it tomorrow. One day's bad luck. Two days of trouble and a man's got to start lookin' for a Jonah. Don't you Jonah me, boy."

I went home. I spent the afternoon and evening trying to convince myself that I had no control over the bad luck of the morning. There was nothing I could have done to change the weather, prevent the glass from breaking, or the fan belt and trotline from snapping. All I had done was catch on rather slowly to Bart's ways of culling crabs. Could that have changed the tone of the morning?

Bart asked me to be aboard by 3:30 the next morning. The weather promised a better day, and Bart had an idea. He had heard that another crabber had caught fifteen bushels in a small bay across the Choptank River. The bay had not been crabbed all summer. Bart was going to abandon his normal lay and try this new ground. He and I would set two lines. Catch crabs enough for two that way.

The trip across the Choptank took more than an hour, but the time passed quickly because Bart and I worked putting bait on the two trotlines. The crabber stored salt eels in an oil drum near the front of the boat. We cut the eels into chunks, tied a chunk to each of the snoods, and dipped the bait into a box of salt before the line was coiled at our feet. At one point in the process of baiting up it seemed like the entire boat was knee deep in trotline, but it was all coiled neatly into barrels before *At Last* reached her destination.

Murphy pointed out a course to me that ran toward the flashing light on a bellbuoy. I steered the boat while Bart talked on the CB to Bucky, the man who had discovered the new lay the day before.

"Hey Buck, where you at?"

"Bellbuoy."

"Can't see you."

"Where you?"

" 'Bout the bellbuoy."

"I see you hoss. Bright as Christmas."

"Flash your lights, Buck."

"No way. Half Tilghman's trying to follow me today. Know what I did yarsterday, and they're all greedy. Goin' to be a sea o' lines down here if them boys see where I'm layin'. Know where I'll be. See you there at sunup."

"Know what you mean," said Bart switching off *At Last*'s running lights. The radio crackled to itself. No bantering with Bucky broke over channel 17, but I sensed that a fleet of boats were seriously in pursuit of us. Red and green running lights speckled the water astern. Bart took the controls, added power.

Just at sunrise *At Last* pulled up beside a shabby little crab skiff with a faded red awning. A young waterman with a thick mustache and lambchop sideburns hardly looked up from watching his line. Dip, dip, dip. He was on a mess of crabs.

"Damn, it's hard findin' this place in the dark, ain't it, Buck? Can't get the smart of it. Not been here for years. Missed something didn't I?" said Bart.

Bucky smiled and kept dipping.

"Ain't goin' to crowd you, Buck. Never layed close to a man's line. Where do you want me to lay?"

I was surprised by the deference in Bart Murphy's voice. There weren't many people Murphy humbled himself to, especially when they were as young as Bucky.

Bucky shrugged his shoulders to Bart's question, "Lay

anywhere along these edges. S'ppose there's plenty crabs. Got three-quarters of a bushel on my first run."

Murphy waved appreciation and pulled *At Last* away from the small skiff, then explained his deference: "One crabbin' son-of-a-bitch, that Bucky is. Find crabs in his sleep, he can. We help each other out. No sense in rivalin' a boy that's got the talent of God."

Bart watched his repaired depth sounder; he had "fixed" it during the long trip across the Choptank. Three whacks from crab tongs and a frenzied twisting of dials had produced a readable signal where there had been none before—so much for modern science. The depth sounder showed that Bucky had laid along a ten-foot edge. Murphy decided to move in shore a couple hundred yards and lay his first line at seven feet—"Could be crabs will move to shoaler water when the current changes in half an hour."

The first line was set without effort. I took care of my chores—leading out the line, setting up the baskets, pouring the captain's coffee—without Murphy's giving a word of direction. It was 6:00 A.M., and the two of us took our shirts off. A breeze blew haze out of the southwest.

"Goin' to show you some crabbin' today," said Murphy.

I smiled, hoped it was so.

"Guess we ought to run this line 'fore we lay our second one. Just to make sure we're on the crabs. What do you think?"

I was shocked that Bart was consulting me. I had no idea what the relationship would be between the first and second lays, so I agreed with Murphy out of a sense of protocol: the captain is always right.

"Well, all right, but . . . maybe we don't need to run this first. Maybe we should watch Buck a bit, see which end o' his line's doin' the most good."

I shrugged. I didn't want to make the decision.

"Alright, c'mon, let's run this one fast," said Murphy. His loud tone suggested that he was trying to convince himself and me.

At Last started down her first lay with more speed than Bart had used the day before. I sat on the roof and watched the line rise over the roller. Crabs appeared erratically. Some dropped off before Murphy ever saw them. The crabber kept shifting his attention from his line to Buck's boat, then back to the line again. Bart made gentle dips into the calm water.

At the end of the run Murphy growled: "Damn, we got thirty-two and Bucky's got forty-five. Got to take her up, lay somewhere better. Don't you think?"

I didn't know. I thought this lay would be fine if we ran it slower and forgot about Bucky. He was going much slower and not dividing his attention between his trotline and another boat.

"Let's take her up," said the captain.

I didn't voice my opinion. I cast my dissenting vote silently for setting the second lay. We could run the first one with more care later.

It took us more than half an hour to haul the line. During the time we worked "taking up" five other Tilghman boats arrived in the small bay. Each boat drifted up alongside *At Last*.

"Not much here," said Murphy to each of the crabbers. "Got to move. Anybody doin' anything?"

The crabbers would shake their heads: "We heard you and Bucky got 'em all for yourselves down here."

"Perty story. But if I got a mess o' crabs you can have 'em."

Murphy held up the catch—a third of a bushel. "Ain't even supper."

The crabbers shook their heads, smiled and motored alongside Bucky. By the time *At Last* had her trotline aboard, all five of the new arrivals were setting lines in the small bay. They set gear at both ends and either side of Bucky. One crabber lay in almost the same spot where *At Last* had just taken up.

"Boys seen what Bucky got; guess they want some o' it. But I don't think they'll catch much. That ten-foot edge where Buck's at got all the crabs. Don't you think?"

I shook my head. I didn't know where the crabs were. I only knew that I had been on the water for more than four hours without establishing the routine of the trotline.

"Watch these boys for awhile," said Murphy, shutting off *At Last*'s engine. It's goin' to tell us where to lay. If you can't read the water, read the crabbers."

For an hour *At Last* drifted. Bart and I counted how many times the other crabbers dipped. An hour survey yielded some facts: Bucky was catching about a half bushel each run. The other boats were catching a quarter to a third of a bushel. If the catch remained consistent, Bucky might have ten bushels for the day. The other men would have four or five apiece.

"Got to have more than five bushels to make a livin'," said Bart.

"Hundred fifty dollars," I said.

"Can't two of us live on that."

"I could try."

"No. Got to find crabs like I had last week. Had 'em on every snood. Maybe we should set out in deeper water 'long these eighteen-foot and fifteen-foot ledges. Might be too warm for most crabs up in the shallows."

I agreed. I didn't care whether Bart's theory made sense: I just wanted to get the lines laid.

Murphy did too. *At Last* set both lines in less than half an hour; the boat planed over the water. The wind cooled us.

The first run produced fifty-nine crabs. The crew of *At Last* stopped watching the other watermen. This was crabbing, and the morning was wearing on. It was almost ten o'clock.

For the next two hours we alternated jobs—driving/dipping or culling—whole bushels of crabs were stacked in the shade of the cabin house. The lay on the eighteen-foot edge averaged a third of a bushel each run, but the fifteen-foot lay caught slightly less. A little after noon Bart asked me if we should take up the trotline on the "poor lay." He said the fifteen-foot lay was a waste of time.

I disagreed. I was tired and a bit belligerent from the long day and hot sun. I figured two lines were better than one. Leave both of them down. It was like having two fish hooks —your chances were better.

"It ain't the same," said Murphy. Maybe he was right. We took up the line and stopped talking. The eighteen-foot edge continued to produce a fair haul of crabs. At 3:30 *At Last* was one of the final boats to reach Tilghman. Bart and I earned $100 each. We went to the bars that night. Different bars.

The rest of the week went much the same way. *At Last* left port early and came home late. In between there was a lot of setting, hauling, and resetting gear. We spent time trying to "read" other crabbers, and we spilled a lot of words over where the crabs were. I found that I was beginning to disagree with Bart just for the sake of argument. Bart began to complain about being unable to pay off boatyard debts. Often there wasn't enough work to keep both of us busy, so we took turns sleeping. Bart and I didn't laugh together anymore.

After a three-bushel catch on Saturday, I told Bart I would look for other work. One man, one trotline—that was the right formula.

The Fourth of July passed. I drifted with a group of dredgers who worked erratically in the summer—"Crab when I feel like it. Paint a boat for someone now and again. Raise hell mostly." The routine of loafing along the waterfront or in bars, around coffee urns, passed the time; it was also a good way to look for a job. Sooner or later someone would need a hand. Word was the clam boats were taking on additional crew.

In late morning I loafed with a group of retired or "part-time" watermen who sat around on crab baskets at the boat basin on Knapps Narrows. Here two old men bought soft crabs from watermen who tied their skiffs in the basin. From here all the news of the day was spread to the community.

Always the first boats in were the clam or "mano" boats, and the arrival of these craft caused a flow of rumor, accusation, and speculation among the men on the wharf.

"Here come that new breed."

"Mudpuppies."

"Weren't but a handful of 'em twenty years ago."

"Now they're thick as nettles."

"Goin' to ruin the arster beds, sure."

"Who invented that silly lookin' rig for diggin' clams out of the mud?"

"Old Fletcher Hanks from Oxford."

"Shit."

"He just see'd a market; I don't blame a man for that."

"No, but ain't a Bayman in his right mind who would eat one of those trash clams. Damn 'fish bait,' that's what I call many nose, 'mano' clams."

"They ain't cherrystones for certain."

"Soft shells is what they is."

"In New England they call 'em 'steamers'."

"Can't get enough of 'em, and now they got the city folk tuned to 'em."

"Seller's market. Man can make more at it than at crabbin'."

"But a crabbin' rig don't cost much and don't tear up the bottom. Mano rig got to cost more than $5,000 and that don't include the boat."

"That's complicated stuff. Got that drudge down there with a high-pressure water system to dig into the mud. Conveyor bringin' up the manos."

"It's an ugly mess, ain't it?"

"The way that conveyor leans out to starboard; sink a boat in a runnin' sea."

"Don't think it hasn't happened."

"I couldn't give a damn; let 'em all sink 'fore they tear up the arster beds we got left."

"They'll do it, too. Mano rigs put deep ruts in the bars so nothin' will grow."

"I don't believe the state would let 'em do it if it was so bad."

"Law says clammers can't work on an arster bar, but Lord if they ain't workin' out there on drudger's ground right now. Marine Police ain't caught 'em yet."

"When's the state ever done anything right by the Bay. Limitin' drudgin' to sailboats is about the smart of it."

"Yea, ask them mano boys. They'll tell you they always got to be findin' new bottom. Old mano bars won't grow neither clam once they been dug up."

"Won't be long 'fore they kill this tired old Bay. Ain't pollution goin' to do it; poor conservation's the bad guy."

"Ain't that bad. These mano boats got a fifteen-bushel limit."

"And don't it get enforced right well, too? Everybody knows at least three clammers on this island that caught more than forty bushels apiece yarsterday."

"Damn. I know it."

"Who bothers them? No one!"

"Can't blame a man for catchin' all he can."

"No, but then why have limits? State boys watch the tongers and drudgers close enough don't they? Ain't all of us paid fines last winter for bein' just a couple of bushels over the limit? Why don't they watch the clammers?"

"Maybe those state boys eat clams."

"That's about as right a reason as you can get."

"It's crazy times we live in."

"Ain't it always so?"

Every day I watched and listened. I wasn't sure how I felt about the ethics of the clam business, but I knew I had less than $300 in my pocket. This is bankruptcy for a waterman.

I began to canvas the wharves. It didn't take long to find a clammer willing to take me on. It was work, and besides I wanted to see if clamming was the "devil industry" the oystermen claimed.

The boat's name was *Mariner* and in the shadows of morning moonlight she looked nothing like the vessels I knew. Unlike the thin swallowtailed skiffs that characterize Chesapeake workboats, *Mariner* was as husky as a Nova Scotian trawler—forty-feet long, fifteen feet broad, high bow, big cabin. Along the right side of the boat hung a conveyor more than thirty-five feet long encased in heavy bridge work. A three-foot wide mouth of dredge teeth marked the forward end. All of this was suspended from two iron trestles by a complex of cables, springs, and pulleys. Hydraulic lines and a fire hose sprawled across the working area, two engines, and iron work.

There was a light in the cabin so I stepped aboard.

A tall black man met me.

"New man," I explained. I extended my hand to shake.

The black grunted and held his ground in the middle of the

boat. He pushed the final third of a thick sandwich into his mouth and stared down at me. As he chewed, something in his mouth crunched.

"Lewis," he said finally. His hand met mine.

"Cap'n's late," said Lewis as he motioned me into the large cabin that was finished in varnish like a yacht. "Have a munchy," he added.

The crewman dipped into what appeared to be a case of snack cakes and tossed a creamed-filled something to me, then served himself. The radio began to chatter on channel 7: something about a man named Joe, who had loaded life jackets aboard a Boston Whaler the previous evening, kept being repeated by different voices.

Lewis smiled and spoke through a mouthful of cake: "Lawman's back. Gonna be some shootin' now. You watch, 'less the mice outsmart the cat."

Lewis saw that he had to explain. Joe was the local Marine policeman. His cabin cruiser had been hauled out for repairs for the past few weeks. With no policeman on the water, some clammers had been digging anywhere they wished—often on off-limit oyster bars—and catching many times their quota. But now rumor was circulating that the policeman had prepared his Boston Whaler skiff to make a raid on the illegal clammers. The radio banter suggested that the clammers were ready.

Lewis chuckled about the clammers' foreknowledge of the police raid: "We got a big ten-twenty on that smokey." He opened another snack cake and pulled a stack of stag magazines from a locker.

"Check it out," said Lewis tossing a pornographic photo essay at me. "Let that mess with your head awhile." Lewis spread a pile of life preservers on the floor of the forepeak, then collapsed on them with his cake and magazine. Within minutes he began to snore.

The captain bounded aboard. In one motion he started *Mariner*'s diesel engine and cast off the stern lines. In the next moment he acknowledged my presence with a nod and a gesture to the bow lines. *Mariner* was moving out of her slip almost before I had thrown her lines clear.

As the boat churned out into the Bay the captain, Russell Dize, steered from the cabin. He wore a numbered sweatshirt and a baseball cap. The clothes and his fine features made the captain look only half of his thirty-five years. The quick way he moved around the cabin adjusting lights, radios, engine controls, and nameless other pieces of electronic equipment added to his youthful appearance.

But the radio chatter froze Dize's attention on the speaker.

"Hey Robby, come back. I seen him."

"Yeah. Go ahead."

"Whaler left the dock at three."

"Some sneakin' sombitch."

"Yeah, I guess he got an ambush planned."

"Where's he at now?"

"Don't know."

Dize keyed his microphone, "Come at me, Robby."

"Yeah, Russell, where you goin'?"

"Now, I guess that depends on the smokey."

"Guess it does. I'll give a call. See who got a current ten-twenty on that whaler."

"OK."

Dize tuned his radio to channel 17 and heard his friend broadcast: "This the Outlaw. Who got bearings on a bald smokey in a mosquito? Come back."

"Running inside Black Walnut Point an hour ago."

"Someone seen smoke at the bellbuoy at 4:30."

"That's a ten-four."

"Outlaw, this is Hawkeye. Go down to zero-five on the express."

Dize spun his tuner to channel 5 and heard the end of the smokey report:

"... drifting in the lee of Sharps Island Light at the present."

"Thank you, Cap. Outlaw off."

Dize switched back to channel 7, the clammers' station, and gave a call, "Hey, Robby."

"Yeah, Russell."

"You hear that smokey report?"

"Yeah, Russell."

"Where you at?"

"Where I ain't suppose to be. How about you?"

"I'm just makin' out; I was comin' to find you."

"Forget that. I'm hot property. Sounds like the heat is on to me. Gonna try to get lost 'fore sunup. Catch you on the flip flop."

"Happy trails."

"Ten-four."

Dize turned to me and frowned: "Damn if I'm goin' to need an extra man when the law's around. We dug up all the legal grounds on Sharp's Island already, but that's where we got to work today. If the law don't see us there he'll know we been up to no good. If we don't hit on a fresh patch among the trenches we already dug, we won't catch enough manos to buy munchies for Lewis."

"Hard times come again," groaned Lewis from the floor. "I seen the future and it's fried arsters and corn meal."

I laughed—just so much down-and-out banter to pass the time.

But the captain didn't laugh. "I'll tell you how bad it is workin' on old clammin' ground. Last time the boys come out here the best thing caught all day was the engine off a Navy fighter plane that crashed. This is a brand new boat. $25,000 if it cost a nickel. Can't pay the bills workin' Sharps Island.

Clams haven't even come back to places we haven't touched for five years."

If the day had stopped here, I would have felt a confirmation of all of the bad rumors about the mano fleet. But suddenly the captain shrugged his shoulders and threw up a grin. No use complaining. Clamming had been a good business. One year in the mid-sixties the Chesapeake clam catch was over a million bushels. The recent catch was significantly less than that, but the price of twenty dollars per bushel still made the hunt for manos attractive.

Dize said clammers didn't like having to work illegally on oyster bars. He said this law-breaking had only become pervasive in the last five years: "Hurricane Agnes brought us to this sneakin' around. Killed all the grass on the bottom of the Bay. Probably the herbicides that the Susquehanna swept into the Chesapeake is what done it."

The clammer explained that clams live in sand bottom or where there is a mixture of sand and mud. Seagrass is what keeps the natural clam beds from being covered by a blanket of choking silt. With the sea grass gone, many natural beds have been overwhelmed by silt and have not given young clams a place to thrive. Clams have settled onto bars protected from siltation by oysters. Some natural clam bars like Sharps Island still produce a good annual yield, but the large clamming fishery, which was developed to farm a Bay that produced a limitless harvest, can sweep the natural beds clean in a fraction of the year. Since many clammers have a large financial investment, and depend on clamming as a year-round occupation, the temptation to poach clams from oyster bars has been strong. For many, occasional poaching has meant the difference between a moderate income and bankruptcy.

"This is the most mechanized waterman's work, and the most expensive. Used to be 'bout the richest job, too. Can't count on that no more," sighed the captain. He had taken to buying clams, crabs, and oysters for selling on the wholesale market in Baltimore to supplement his income. Lewis helped in that enterprise, too.

"Through thick and thin, we been. Ain't it, Russell?" mumbled Lewis from the floor.

"He's talkin' 'bout his waistline, I guess," teased the captain. "Unless the state gets busy resurveying the bottom of this Bay, 'stead of counting on a 1907 study to tell 'em where the legal oyster and clam bars are, they'll have to change Lewis's nickname from 'Big Daddy' to 'Slim'."

"Horseshit!" cried Lewis.

"Yeah, clammin's goin' to hell; they'll make a drudger out of you, Lewis."

"Believe I won't do nothin' on a drudge boat but cook. Rest is common nigger work. Ain't I got more civil rights than that?"

"Won't argue that," said the captain, "least 'til we trim 'bout 150 pounds from your black hide."

"Dream on, white man," chuckled Lewis. He addressed me: "You see whose lyin' down and whose workin', don't you? That's the natural order of things."

"Your chance is comin', boy," countered the captain. He aimed *Mariner* at lights bobbing on the Bay.

It was sunrise when *Mariner* reached the legal clamming grounds on Sharps Island. More than fifty other boats floated in the same area. They shut off their engines and drifted. The captains and crew yelled greetings, "Lord, if it don't look like a convention."

"Goin' to put on a right legal show for the law, ain't we?"

"Be a good show of poverty, as many clams as we're goin' to catch here."

"Maybe the man will feel sorry for us and go home."

"Damn if they won't send an airplane out to watch, then; them oystermen been complainin' too loud."

"Looks bad; might find a lump, though."

"Yeah, guess we'll start lookin'."

Russell Dize turned the ignition switch on *Mariner*; nothing happened. The battery was dead. A frown came over the captain's face. He roused Lewis. Lewis fetched gallons of battery water from a Jerry jug. Dize climbed down into the boat's deep bilges and slowly filled the cells of a battery.

After twenty minutes, Dize tried the ignition. Nothing happened. He swore and called to a nearby boat for help—a jump start. Meanwhile Lewis went into the cabin and turned off two radios, lights, tape deck, and depth sounder. Then he tried the starter on the small donkey engine that drove the pumping system in the clam rig. The engine turned over. It generated enough to start the big diesel.

"Hey, ain't I lucky?" said Lewis.

"Yeah, you're almost white," Dize said.

The captain manipulated three hydraulic controls mounted near the wheel at the stern of *Mariner*. The conveyor lowered until its dredge end caught on the bottom. Lewis engaged the pump; the fire hose swelled and drove pressurized water through a nine-hole nozzle on the head of the dredge. The gush of water and the dredge teeth began tearing a rut in the bottom twelve inches deep and thirty-six inches wide. The boat crept ahead. The conveyor turned. Lewis and I stood near the stern of the boat and picked clams from the mass of mud, rocks, and old shells that shuttled up the conveyor. Lewis put cotton in his ears to black out the roar of the engines and machinery. An assembly line rhythm took hold of us—pick-a-clam-and-rest, pick-a-clam-and-rest. Large manos, the size of peaches, were culled into one bucket, smaller clams went into another.

"Least we'll get our limit here!" shouted the captain over the din. Just then the fire hose ruptured and began thrashing around *Mariner*. Lewis dove for the pump switch and cut the power to the machinery before more than a few dozen gallons had doused us and poured into the boat.

Dize turned on me: "Two breakdowns and the law all in one morning. Never broke a hose before, never had a battery die. Damn if Bart Murphy didn't warn me, boy. You put a Jonah on us. Like to throw you overboard." Dize's face showed no expression; I didn't think he was teasing. Was I carrying bad luck? Would I be looking for a job again? I had heard the men at the wharf say the reputation of a Jonah could kill a man in Tilghman.

I helped Lewis drag a trunk of tools from *Mariner*'s cabin. When we faced the captain again, Lewis spoke up: "Let's put the Jonah off on the lighthouse, Cap. Let the smokey pick him up. That ought to fix things right." The black slapped me on the back: it meant he was joking.

"Suppose it's not a bad idea," I said dejectedly. "My luck could sink that lawman."

The captain smiled back: "Forget it, kid. All this machinery means that breakdowns are half the life of a clammer. Hand me a $\frac{9}{16}''$ socket wrench; we'll get this back together in a jiffy." A half hour later the hose was spliced together with a joint made from a length of $3''$ pipe and two hose clamps. The parts had been carried for just such an emergency.

Mariner's dredge began to plow along the bottom again, but few clams appeared on the conveyor. Dize, Lewis, and I stood side-by-side and watched trash churn up the conveyor.

"Damn, if we ain't lost that patch," said the captain. He wrenched the hydraulic levers and the dredge rose from the water. *Mariner* steamed toward a fleet of other clammers.

At least fifteen boats spread out in a line. They moved north across the water in formation. Dize lowered *Mariner*'s rig.

"Keep watchin' those other boats," said the captain to me. "See how much pickin' they do. If a boat gets onto a fresh patch you'll see right quick. They'll be pickin' their hands off."

I nodded and watched the other boats. There was little work on my own conveyor.

"What we're doin' now is prospectin'. Any one of the boats gets on a good patch, we'll all come back to it—course, if it's small, the finder's got his rights. Clammers are pretty good about helpin' each other. Got to stick together 'cause there's so many against us that . . ."

The dredge began to shudder.

"Sweet Mama, ain't we onto something," said Lewis coming out of a trance. "Look there," he pointed down the conveyor. Large brown oysters rose from the water.

"Where's the law, Cap?"

"He ain't none too far away."

"Can I shuck 'em?"

"Not this mornin', not with our luck. Lawman be here 'fore you cleaned a dozen shells. Goin' to play by his rules today: law says you can't have neither oyster on a clam rig. We won't have a one. Let 'em tumble back, Lewis. Don't even touch that conveyor. The man got his binoculars on you this minute."

"Go to hell," said the black to me. "Slow days like this when we get onto some arsters, I usually shuck out a few. Fry a mess up for lunch. But guess we'd get our bottoms wooped today. Damn if an arster ain't a right eatin' thing. Make clams taste common." He expressed a popular Chesapeake prejudice.

Clams appeared with such scarcity that the captain and

Lewis disappeared into the cabin to split some snack cakes and talk to their friends on the CB. I watched while the machinery turned over the bottom and found it lacking. Over a speaker mounted near the controls at the stern of the boat, I heard part of the CB conversation. No clammer had more than a couple bushels on board. The Marine Police officer had boarded a lot of boats.

Mariner traveled with the prospecting fleet for an hour, but when nothing of any significance was turned up, Russell Dize went searching for some patches that had yielded well ten years before. After two hours of searching relatively barren ground, Dize found one of his patches. The conveyor filled with clam shells, but the clams were all dead or dying—"boxes." The most interesting thing scraped from the bottom was a live fifty-caliber machine-gun shell, a legacy from the days when Sharps Island was a target range for Navy aircraft.

Mariner continued to hunt and gather until noon when state law says summer clamming must end. The vessel had caught only eight bushels of manos. It was the first time Dize had failed to catch his limit all summer. It was the same story on many other clam boats.

The captain said he wasn't calling me the Jonah; he said he was blaming the law. The state should resurvey the bottom and find beds where the mano boats could catch legal clams. With no new beds, and aggressive policing, the clammers were in trouble. "It's gettin' to the place where a man must decide whether he wants to break the law, risking fines and court, or go broke and hungry."

"Be a nigger's life soon enough," said Lewis.

As *Mariner* entered the harbor, she overtook Bart Murphy's crab boat. Russell Dize held up eight fingers, then pointed to me.

Murphy began to laugh and shake his head, "Didn't I tell

you, Russell? Ain't goin' to catch either thing while that boy puts a Jonah on you."

I threw a clam at Murphy to show I could take the joke.

"Listen, I'm goin' to tell you what you need," continued Bart. "Got to get yourself one of these." Murphy hoisted a blond boy onto the engine box; it was Bart's three-year-old son, Little Bart. "Best luck in the world. We caught twelve bushels today. This boy is the thing o' my life."

The boats found their separate wharves. *Mariner*'s crew split the last snack cake.

The Marine Police watched the clammers closely during the remainder of July. There was no work clamming. I joined the basket sitters along Knapps Narrows.

"Hey, boys, I'm goin' to give a Jonah another chance. What do you think?" The voice was Bart Murphy's. The crabber passed bottles of Michelob around to the basket sitters.

"Been doin' well, have you, Bart?" asked an old man.

"Was havin' right fair days, Cap'n Willie. You know what I mean—eight or twelve baskets of good ones. Been takin' Little Bart with me. Boy picks up a crab like it were a toy. But I ain't doin' much now. Crabs dropped off. I'm goin' to the railway tomorrow . . . if Randy will help me."

Murphy stared into his beer and talked about me as if he were shy. It was a side of the waterman I had forgotten during the difficult days of crabbing with him. Bart wanted to restore the friendship. I did too.

I tried to say something casual and provocative: "Goddamn, if a man wants my help and can't look me in the eye and ask for it, he must be a sissy baby. How's he ever goin' to get my attention, Bart?" I surprised myself with the way the words rolled from my tongue.

"Smack you 'longside the head. Show you right now who's a jackass and a sissy baby." Murphy threw an exaggerated right hook at my head.

I let the punch land: "If that's all the strength you got, then I guess you need help. Doesn't look like I've got anything better to do."

"Then I guess we'd better drink another beer, hadn't we?"

I walked to Gary's station for a sixpack. I couldn't risk being a Jonah again.

As the men sat in the shade of an old tin building, Bart explained his plans. The Bay Country Festival was being held in Cambridge on the next weekend. The highlight of the weekend was the Saturday evening workboat races. Bart wanted to win. Even more than that, he wanted to beat his brother and a couple of other old rivals. It would take Bart and me the next five days to get *At Last* ready for her challenge.

"See Irving's putting a new engine in," said one of the basket sitters.

" 'Deed he is. They say she'll turn 6500."

"That ain't no workin' motor: she'd overheat if he tried to run a trotline with her."

"I don't think she'll go slow enough to work."

"I'll tell you what," said Bart. "It ain't no workin' rig, but let him run. I got plans and I don't want to hear old Irving bitchin' about souped-up engines, no more."

"Last year he got them Kent Island boys disqualified 'cause he said they weren't workboats."

"Honey, you bet he did. Now isn't he doing the same thing —buildin' a racer—by puttin' in this new motor?"

"What the hell, let 'em all run, I say. I got something that just might put it on 'em."

"What you got, Bart?"

The crabber looked left and right. He made sure the wharf was clear of informers. Then he bent his head down and looked at the basket sitters as if he were peering over the rims of a pair of eyeglasses, "Got STP!"

"In your motor? That ain't nothin'. Put it in my wife's old Ford."

"It's for the bottom," said Murphy.

"What?"

"Me and Randy goin' to paint STP on the bottom of the boat just before we put her overboard for the race."

"I never heard o' such a thing."

"Slicker'n eels," smiled Bart. "Them boys down in Georgia use it on their crab boats and they say it saves 'em six or seven gallons of gas a day. Now you know that stuff's got to be doin' some greasin'."

" 'Deed it must."

"STP, um hum. Sounds crazy."

"My secret weapon. Now don't either one of you let it out. I'm takin my boat the whole way over to St. Michaels to haul out on the railway so these island boys don't know what me and Randy are doin'. There's no one goin' to call Randy a Jonah after this race."

The next day Bart Murphy ran *At Last* over to a St. Michaels boatyard. A host of Tilghman Islanders had driven there to meet him. Everyone stood in the blistering heat and watched a travel lift sling *At Last* out of the water and onto wooden chocks.

"Let's get the floor and gear out of her, boys," called Murphy as he mounted the beached vessel. "Let that sun dry her out, lighten her up."

"In minutes the watermen had stripped *At Last* of everything removable and stowed the items in the back of several pickups.

Local watermen and visiting yachtsmen were attracted by the gang who stood around *At Last* eyeing her hull lines, swiveling her rudder, and fingering her propeller.

"Right hollow wheel [propeller] you got there, Bart."

"That's just the old 19/19 I used on her for last year's race. Them boys at the prop shop are makin' up a new wheel for me right now. Goin' to have more cup to her."

"Wheel'll make all the difference."

" 'Deed it will. I'm goin' to tell you a thing. I had a bad wheel on this boat one year and she wouldn't do nothin'. Motor turned more than 4,500, but honey, she wouldn't go twenty-five miles per hour." Murphy shook his head as if the memory made him angry.

The eyeing of *At Last* continued. Questions flowed. Beer spilled. More than two dozen people milled around. Bart gave his secret of STP again. I wondered what I contributed to the afternoon. Bart had his admirers. They all pledged to help prepare *At Last*.

But only I was there the next afternoon to sand and paint the workboat's bottom. Sanding by hand took three hours. Flecks of red copper paint stuck to my body and made me itch. Paint chips and sandpaper grit kept falling into my eyes and mouth. I understood why watermen called painting a boat's underside the "worst job in the business."

Bart had gone crabbing with his cousin and arrived at the boatyard after I had finished sanding *At Last*. I had just begun painting.

"Damn, I see you didn't let me down, this time. Guess them other fellows is sissy babies, don't you? Afraid to crawl under a boat and get dirty."

"Or maybe they're just smarter," I said.

"Then I like bein' dumb," said the captain, grabbing a paint roller and ducking under the boat beside me.

"Yeah, it's honest work."

"When you got a pal," said Bart.

"Yeah, Bunk."

Murphy laughed at my attempt at an Eastern Shorism. The work went quickly.

The day before the race Bart and I had *At Last* looking as trim and bright as a yacht. Only a few things remained to be done. We had to buy high octane airplane fuel, add the new propeller, tune the engine, and apply the STP. Bart arranged for a mechanic, mounted the new propeller, and ran the mission for special fuel with a "nitro" additive. I started painting on STP.

Back in Tilghman word of Murphy's secret weapon had already touched off a controversy. The secret had filtered out to the community through the basket sitters:

"I think he's bluffin'."

"Yessir, so do I: STP is too sticky. Like to stop you dead."

"But I seen a case of it in the back o' Bart's truck."

"He'll use it. You can bet on it."

"They say it makes them Georgia crabbers faster."

"Who says? Maybe just Bart Murphy says. Maybe he's just tryin' to worry his brother and these other fellas."

" 'Deed, he's done it. I can tell you two other men who got cases of the gunk just ready."

"Don't know whether to put it on or not. Won't neither one of 'em get it near to a boat hull 'fore they know certain that Bart done it."

"Old Bart's got 'em goin'."

"Yes sir, but them others'll find out. They got spies."

"Lot o' *do* for a five-minute race."

"Lot o' money. You know some o' these boys have spent more than $500 gettin' ready."

"Honey, it's more fuss than a boat full o' loose crabs."

That was what I was thinking as I dipped my roller in the honey-like STP and stroked it onto *At Last*. The lubricant was so cohesive that it threatened to make the roller stick to the boat. Tacky drops spit at me as the roller snapped and bubbled over the boat hull. When I tried to wipe the STP off myself, the grease refused to lift. It smeared.

On Friday evening watermen from St. Michaels and Tilghman gathered around *At Last* to evaluate Bart's progress and see his secret weapon. Everyone seemed to bring a friend. One group of Tilghman men brought several carpenters and mechanics from a rival boatyard. The rivals pretended to be busy examining several workboats that were for sale near *At Last*, but they kept glancing toward Bart's boat and talking in low tones to each other. Sometimes the rivals seemed to eavesdrop on the conversation that *At Last* generated.

These conversations gained momentum as I rolled on the last strokes of STP.

"Lord, that stuff looks bad, Bart. You sure its goin' to make you faster?"

"It does look kind o' bubbly, don't it?" Murphy picked up a clean paint brush and began trying to stroke bubbles out of the STP. He pressed hard with the paint brush, but thousands of tiny bubbles dotted the lubricant.

"Maybe it will smooth out when you get her movin'."

"Or maybe it will make him stick to the water like this." A waterman pressed his thumb to *At Last*'s bow and pulled it away with a pop. STP stretched like cobwebs between the hull and the thumb.

Men laughed. Bart coughed nervously.

I came to the defense of the secret weapon. I had only a basic idea of the physics of STP, but I had an investment in time, energy, and body abuse in Bart's idea.

"This stuff reduces friction in motors, doesn't it? Why won't it work on a boat hull?" I began.

" 'Cause motors is hot, boats ain't, boy."

"You sure?"

"Ain't never burned my hand on the bottom of a boat," replied a thin old waterman I didn't know.

"Maybe not," I said, "but a hull moving through the water at twenty-five miles per hour has got to cause a lot of friction. STP reduces friction. It'll make the water run by the boat better and . . ."

Water from a garden hose blasted me in the chest. "Don't see that water runs off your greasy body any better," said one of the STP's detractors. "Seems to stick on you."

Large beads of water hung from my oil-soaked skin. I couldn't explain the apparent stickiness of the STP. I thought it might be a good time to go home, before I got into a fight.

As I drove out of the boatyard I could hear the rival boatyard specialists telling Bart that he had blown it. Better get some kerosene and wipe all the STP off. Bart shook his head as if he were punch drunk and gulped a seven-ounce Michelob in one swallow.

I rose early the day of the races and called Bart's house: Bart and I had to help Ronnie, a mechanic Bart called the best engine man on the Eastern Shore, to tune *At Last*'s Cadillac V-8. Bart wasn't home, his wife said, wearily. Was he at the boat? Must be: he hadn't come home last night. Must have gotten drunk.

At Last had been lowered into the water by the time I arrived at the boatyard. She floated in a bay beneath the travel lift. The slings of the lift dangled into the water and made loops under the workboat. Ronnie and Bart crouched over the engine. Murphy's clothes were soiled with sweat and grease. His hair and beard glistened with oil. Had he scrubbed off the STP, or was Bart bathed in sweat?

Before I even greeted the men I bent down into the travel lift bay and reached out to touch *At Last* below the waterline.

"Goddamn if it isn't the Jonah come to see if his curse is still on us, Ronnie. 'Deed it's still there, boy. Damn, if I didn't try to wash it off with a bucket full o' beers last night, but it was still there this mornin'. 'Put her overboard' I told the yard boys. Hell with the STP. If she slows me down I'm goin' to tell 'em: 'Randy done it.' With your bad luck won't be a person who thinks otherwise."

"I'm not worried," I said. "I don't have to explain to your wife why you never made it home last night." I was taking advantage of Bart's hangover. "Oh God," said Murphy. "What'd she say when you talked to her?"

"Said she was mad enough to box your ears, but she still planned on going to the races."

"That's Florence, ain't it?" Murphy chuckled. "She's guts. Liable to hit me in front of everyone. Got her rights, I guess."

"I guess so too," said the mechanic. "I'm about to do it myself. Here, Randy, empty this crankcase oil. Look at it. And this oil filter. Stuff's like mud. Damn, Bart, I'm surprised this motor still turns. When'd you change the oil last?"

"You ought to know, you did it," laughed Bart, "for the races last year."

"God, I hope Florence does box your ears, as much care as you take of things. Look at you, you're a grubby mess. Slept in your clothes."

"Fix the engine, Ronnie. I'll get my sermon soon enough."

"Expect you will. Want a beer?"

"What for?"

"Celebrate the STP special. Andy Granatelli is like to have you on TV." The mechanic winked at me.

"Just fix the motor, boys. There's no drinkin' today unless Randy's secret weapon wins us a race. Give me a soda pop. I'm dry." Murphy wiped perspiration from his forehead with an oily hand.

Three hours later *At Last* coasted out into St. Michaels

harbor. The engine had a completely new electrical system. It burned airplane fuel and "nitro" from a five-gallon can on the floor. We had removed the exhaust pipes, and even with the Cadillac idling *At Last* sounded ready for competition at the drag strip. Her growl turned people's heads in the harbor. She was going out for a trial, and I had added a pint of STP to the engine's fresh racing oil. I leaned on the washboards proudly: I had a personal stake in this.

Ronnie leaned over the engine and watched a tachometer and dwellmeter. As *At Last* idled into Miles River past the entrance markers of the harbor, the mechanic signaled Bart with thumbs up. The throttle opened, the engine whined, *At Last*'s bow lifted high out of the water, and walls of spray flared around the hull. For fifteen seconds the boat accelerated across the water. I hung onto the washboards for support, Ronnie watched his gauges and adjusted the four-barrel carburetor with a screwdriver: Bart stood stiffly at the wheel. He alternated his glances between the river and a loose speedometer braced between his feet. When the mechanic smiled and signaled for Bart to slow down the waterman frowned.

"5000 r.p.m.'s. That's 300 more then we got last year!" screamed the mechanic.

"Only twenty-five miles per hour though!" Bart yelled over the popping of the engine.

"Don't believe it. Hit her again," yelled the engine man.

At Last bucked and broke into a sprint again. I held on. The mechanic watched his gauges and smiled. Murphy watched the speedometer and shook his head angrily. To my senses *At Last* seemed to continue accelerating, but the speedometer needle pegged on twenty-five. Murphy wheeled the boat back toward the harbor and slowed down.

"Goddamn it's that STP," he said. "She ain't doin' nothin'. Did twenty-seven miles last year."

"Like hell," countered the mechanic. "This is a different speedometer than you had before. It's never been calibrated. I swear to you we were doin' a lot faster than twenty-five."

Murphy shook his head: "Goddamn Jonah, Goddamn STP. We ain't goin' to do much."

I was too exhilarated from the speed to be discouraged by Murphy's words. I listened to the mechanic's optimism and saw the excited waves people gave *At Last* as she returned to harbor.

We showered, shaved, and left for Cambridge in mid-afternoon. Bart, Ronnie, and I rode without trying to speak over the roar of *At Last*'s engine. Ronnie and I sought shade in the cabin. Bart stood at the wheel and drank orange soda. He seemed to be going over things in his mind: the validity of the speedometer, the news that his adversary with the special racing engine had withdrawn from the race because of mechanical problems, the rumor that four other boats had chosen to copy Murphy's STP treatment. The waterman's mood was hard to read. The skin of his face was stiff with tension as he steered up the Choptank River to Cambridge. But he had shown confidence to the basket sitters at the wharf before leaving Tilghman:

"How's she doin' Bart, how's that secret weapon?"

"She's right as she's ever been, boys. Got the motor turnin' better than either year—5000."

The Bay Country Festival was on a peninsula next to the Yacht Club on the edge of Cambridge. *At Last* was the first workboat to arrive, but within fifteen minutes ten workboats were rafted together along the wharf. Colored lights sprinkled the amusement rides. A ferris wheel turned. Calliope music drifted from a merry-go-round. A crowd gathered. They eyed the watermen and repeated their questions:

"Which boat is from Kent Island?"

"Which boat's from Hoopers Island?"

"Them Tilghman boys is the ones to beat, ain't they?"

"What's your secret, Cap?"

Most of the watermen sat in their boats drinking beer and answering the crowd's questions.

The competitors eyed each other. Bart was quick to spot the sheen of STP on the hull of his brother Wade's boat. Men noted the can of "nitro" racing fuel additive tucked next to *At Last*'s gas cans. Everyone turned his head when a small workboat pulled alongside the group. The new arrival was as lightly built as a runabout and was powered by a new 300 horsepower outboard. The words "That ain't no workboat" eddied among the traditional boats and crews. Some men complained about the outboard, others shrugged—"Let him race unlimited class. Everyone knows that outboard ain't made for workin'."

Women and families joined the watermen aboard the boats. People picked steamed crabs; women complained and laughed about how seriously the men took this race. Florence Murphy smiled at her husband. Bart and I greased *At Last*'s throttle cable; the loudspeaker barked, "Line 'em up, boys. Workboat competition will begin."

The competition was divided into three races. First boats under thirty-eight feet raced around the two-mile oval course. Then boats over thirty-eight feet. Finally, all boats were eligible to compete in the unlimited class free-for-all. This was the event that meant the most to the watermen. It allowed for the settlement of personal grudges, rivalries, and showdowns.

At Last was the only boat racing in the thirty-eight-feet-and-under class. This was the faster class, and the carnival promoters were disappointed that Bart Murphy's competition had failed to appear. Some people said that rumors of Murphy's week-long preparation and secret weapon had scared his competition away. Bart was undaunted: "Hell, just as soon win this class race trophy and seventy-five dollars by scarin' them other fellas away as beat 'em racin'. Save my motor for the unlimited race."

When the handkerchief dropped, Murphy coasted around the race course at three-quarter the racing speed carrying ten people. The crowd applauded politely. They thought they had been ripped off.

At Last tied along the wharf and Bart's passengers unloaded to watch the nine-boat competition for the Second Division trophy. By the time Bart and I had climbed to the top of a truck to get a view, the fleet was just rounding the halfway buoy. Bart's brother jockeyed with a boat from Hoopers Island. Wade Murphy lengthened his lead on the turn, but the Hoopers Island boat began chewing up Wade's lead on the final straightaway. At the finish line Wade Murphy won by less than a boatlength.

"Damn, Wade was movin' better than that old battleship's ever done before," said Bart through his teeth. I could see Bart's jaw muscles bulge as if he were angry or tense. "Hell, if we ain't got some work to do." Murphy jumped from the truck and into *At Last* with only a skip over the wharf.

"Cast off the lines," called Bart to several of the watermen who had ridden in the first race.

The men cast off the lines and prepared to step aboard. Murphy waved them back onto the wharf with a slash of his hand.

"Can't take you, only Randy. Come on, boy. We're goin' to see if you're a Jonah once and for all. Make that secret weapon work." Murphy cupped his hands, spit into them as if he were calling for luck in craps.

The engine beat loudly.

"Stand right front of that motor. Hold on. When I tell you

I want you to, hold that carburetor wide open. Don't let up 'til we cross the finish line," said Bart.

I braced myself on the generator and reached over the spinning fanbelts to the carburetor. I tried to stretch my arm between the vee of cylinders so that if the engine exploded my arm might be spared.

At Last circled in the starting basin with nine other boats. A man standing on the roof of the committee boat one-eighth of a mile ahead motioned the workboats to move toward the starting line. Bart slipped into the pole position beside the outboard. The boats revved their engines like dragsters. Murphy kept flexing his jaw muscles and staring down the line of boats at his brother. Suddenly Murphy ripped the speedometer from the cable at his feet and threw the instrument overboard.

The starter dropped a handkerchief. I jammed the carburetor open. Engines roared. Spray burst from around the boats. Thousands of spectators cheered as the boats boiled past the carnival grounds.

At Last and the outboard were a boatlength ahead of the fleet as they crossed the starting line. Bart kept glancing over at his brother and flexing his jaws. *At Last* continued accelerating. Halfway to the turning buoy the tune of the engine and rushing water seemed to stop changing pitch. The outboard pulled ahead. The rest of the fleet fell several boatlengths behind. Murphy paid no attention to the outboard as he wheeled *At Last* through the turn. He looked back at his brother and his jaw began to relax. I pushed hard on the open throttle.

As the boats moved down the home stretch the noise and speed grew more familiar to me: things seemed to move in slow motion. I saw Bart pirouette at the wheel, stretch out his arms above his head and give an almost endless Bronx cheer to his brother and the rest of the fleet. When Murphy swung back around toward me, a grin stretched across his face, his chest swelled, his head arched back on his neck, and soundless laughter rolled from his mouth.

"That's all I wanted to do," screamed Murphy. "Just wanted to beat my brother. Just wanted to beat Wadie!"

When *At Last* crossed the finish, Bart was still laughing. He shook my hand: "We beat all the workboats there was. Forget that outboard. You and me and STP. Ain't neither bit o' Jonah in you now."

My luck changed. The basket sitters at the wharf made much of Bart Murphy's victory at the Cambridge workboat races. My name was mixed in with this tale of good fortune. Men who had shied from my company began greeting me when they passed on the street. Part-time crabbers were eager for my help. Clammers, driftnetters, crab potters, sport fishermen, and seafood buyers said they could find work for someone who had cast off a Jonah with such a flourish. I had more job offers than I could use. I began to pick my weather, boats, and skippers carefully. I avoided jobs I disliked. I worked only when conditions seemed most promising. I began to learn the art of cultivating a good reputation.

There was one crab potter who attracted my attention. His name was Danny Lednum. He was twenty years old. Everyday when I gathered with the basket sitters, I saw the young crabber make port, watched the slender man swing bushels of crabs onto the wharf. The waterman always wore an oilskin apron and deepwading boots—that he moved so gracefully in spite of them fascinated me.

His face did not look like a Tilghman waterman's: his skin seemed too fair. He marked his homecoming with a silent wave and smile to his fellows.

"Danny's a peach," said one old waterman. "None finer. Wish my boys had grown up like him."

Danny Lednum's catch was rarely exceptional, but the basket sitters said he made money. He worked hard, and he almost always worked alone. Danny was building a nest egg to get married. He was making payments on his boat.

On a Saturday morning in early August I did not report for work. I had spent several days helping an old trotliner work two lays in Broad Creek, but when I woke at 4:30 for crabbing I couldn't keep Broad Creek or trotlining on my mind.

At nine o'clock I walked down to the water to visit the basket sitters. Their seats were empty. The men crowded around the open cab doors of a pickup. A CB chattered from the truck. It was Miss Attie Wood's voice.

"Please clear channel 17. Please clear channel 17. We have an emergency. Repeat, we have an emergency. Leave channel 17 open for emergency communication only."

"Don't this beat hell," began someone in the crowd. "Of all the common sons of bitches that work on the water, why in God's name let this happen to such a good . . ."

The siren at the fire station began. The faces on the men turned blank. Dogs threw their heads back and howled.

"Poor ole Danny," said a bass voice when the siren ceased.

"Of all the ones to get overboard, why Danny?"

"Queerest thing, his motor was shut off."

"He can't swim a lick."

"None of the Lednums can."

"It ain't deep water where they seen his boat driftin'."

"Could be he's got ashore to Poplar Island. I know'd more than one fellow who's got knocked overboard who fetched up on them shoal islands."

"Lord have mercy."

"Yes sir, we better go out and help 'em search."

From the radio: "What was the boy wearin', Miss Attie? Can you call his home and find out?"

I answered the question from memory before Attie Wood could confirm it—deep waders and an oilskin apron.

"I'm afraid for any fella who gets overboard in waders," said one of the men gathered around the pickup. "Water presses them to your legs like concrete. There's no floatin' 'til you get 'em off."

"It don't look good, best take sets of crabpot drags. Let's get goin'. They'll need us."

All along Knapps Narrows men began climbing into workboats. On each boat men carried a handful of foot-long metal tongs laced on to seventy to one hundred feet of line—crabpot drags. They could find a missing crab trap or anything else lost on the bottom of the Bay.

Three of my dredging friends took a skiff they used for part-time crabbing. They talked: "Damn, I think I'd rather be goin' out lookin' for my own father than for Danny."

"Have I lost him, I keep askin'?"

"Christ, if it couldn't be either one of us out there instead of Danny. I'm scared like it was."

"Ain't nothin' wrong with bein' scared."

The skiff carried the three men out into the Poplar Island channel. Already at least two dozen crabpotters, trotliners, clammers, driftnetters, and sport fishing boats clustered around a Marine Police cruiser. More than twenty additional boats headed out of the Narrows to the crabpotting grounds. Rain fell in brief showers.

The police directed a number of boats to check the shores of Poplar and Coach Islands. A private plane flown by a Tilghman seafood buyer began combing the water on the western side of Bay Hundred Peninsula. The rest of the boats spread out between the rows of crab pots. They began a mile or so down the Bay from where Danny Lednum's boat was found. In the stern of each boat watermen held the towline for a drag. The drags were towed in small circles. When nothing was found within the circle made by the dragline, the drag was hauled, then reset on an univestigated patch of bottom.

The airplane and the expedition to the islands turned up nothing. The Saint Michaels Fire Department airboat retraced a path through the marshes repeatedly, but found nothing. The draggers circled slowly into the tide.

Channel 17 spread the story of Danny Lednum. He was to be married in two weeks. There had been a bridal shower for Danny's fiancée last night. He had been in good spirits and more talkative than usual—anxious about the wedding, people guessed. Happy, too, because he had just paid off his boat ahead of schedule. He had left home for work at 5:00 as usual. Everything seemed normal. A number of crabbers had seen Danny pulling pots. Then at about 9:30 several watermen noticed Danny's boat drifting. When they investigated, he was gone.

After two hours of dragging the men began to give in to the idea that sooner or later the search was going to find a corpse. The watermen began to speculate and to reconstruct in minute detail Danny Lednum's last moments.

It was the same kind of speculation I had heard the day after the *Claude W. Somers* had gone down with all hands:

"What do you think got Danny overboard?"

"Don't believe it was a heart attack."

" 'Deed it wasn't; he was as healthy as a colt."

"Queer that motor was shut off."

"So it don't seem possible that a crab pot could have pulled him in."

"No, it don't. He was too careful for that."

"Must o' slipped off the washboard when he was pilin' pots on the stern."

"Probably hit his head and got knocked out."

"He ain't that clumsy."

"Then what got him?"

"I'm goin' to tell you just how it was. He'd been movin' a bunch o' pots—you saw how they was stacked on the stern of his boat. Well, he got 'em all on board, and it was a little after nine o'clock. Danny was hot from pullin' and stackin' all those pots. What would you do? Shut off the motor and take your supper. That's what Danny did. He turned her off and went into the cabin. Got himself a soda and his sandwiches. Then he went out, sat down on the motor box and started to eat. Probably look around a bit to see if the other crab potters were doin' anything. Listenin' to Miss Attie and all. You know how it is. So while he's doin' all this, the boat sets side to the waves. Then he sees a big yacht steamin' by throwin' up one hell of a wake. What would you do?"

"Think about keepin' those crab pots from goin' overboard in the swell of that yacht."

"Right. That's what Danny did. Jumped up on the washboard, sandwich in his hand and all. Tried to brace the pots. Course if the boat hadn't been side to the swell, wouldn't made neither bit o' difference. But anyway that yacht's swell hit him too damn hard. The pots shifted and pushed him overboard."

"And the waders just drug him down."

"Now you know it weren't just the waders."

"Boy couldn't swim. You ever see a person go overboard who can't swim?"

"They don't float neither second. They start to flail and scream. Terrorized, they are. That's what kills 'em. Their body gets so tense they sink and fill with water."

"And that's what happened to Danny."

" 'Fraid it is. Boy probably wasn't more'n five feet from the boat. Couldn't make it. Screamed his lungs out. That drowned him. Panic. Goddamn, I can hear him now, bellowin' like . . ."

"Shut up. Just shut the hell up. I got something on the drag. Slow her down. Give a hand."

The boat slowed. The three men began gently pulling on the drag line. It felt like they had hooked an old mattress. The line came aboard. Hand over hand.

The line went slack.

"Shit, we lost him." There was relief in the voice.

The young men's tugging had attracted attention; several boats came alongside. Something was here. The boats laid their drag lines close to each other. Once again the crew hooked something.

"Feels lighter—like a crabpot. I can get it by myself," said the man reeling in the line.

Caught on the end of one of the drag hooks was a black wading boot.

"Is it his?"

"Now how do I know?"

"We're goin' to have to tell 'em we found this. Get on the radio."

The word spread. Attie Wood relayed the message to Danny's family. A discussion followed between Danny Lednum's family and the men on the water. Was the boot black or brown, old or new? What size was it? There were long pauses in the dialogue. It was Danny's boot.

The drags were laid out again. Some men wanted to believe that finding the free boot was a hopeful sign, but they ignored the description of a drowning man. It wasn't the boots that got a nonswimmer. And what could that heavy thing on the drag have been if it wasn't . . .?

"They got him." The cry came from another boat.

Danny's uncle leaned over the side of his boat and held the black oilskin apron on the body of his nephew.

"That poor son-of-a-bitch," said someone on the radio.

"Goddamn this Bay," said another.

It was three days before Danny Lednum's funeral. A stationary warm front brought thick clouds over Bay Hundred. Surface winds stirred to fifteen knots, then died suddenly. The sky threatened thunder squalls but none struck. Watermen stopped work regularly to listen to the rumble of thunder.

Along the wharves no one raised his voice. The rivalries between watermen and buyers, clammers and oystermen, seemed held in abeyance. Men stared at each other, called their worst enemies "pal." An unusual number of women and children joined watermen at work. Everywhere people recounted the story of Danny Lednum. Each person told his personal memories of the boy's death:

"I couldn't bear to look when they hauled him out."

"I was sick."

"I heard the dogs carryin' on and I knowed."

"Broke my heart to hear 'em tell on the radio."

"I saw that poor girl he was to marry, what could I say?"

"It's always the best the Lord takes young."

On the day of Danny's funeral the streets filled with families walking toward the church. Even the children wore suits and dresses and tried to ignore the 100-degree heat and the grumble of thunder overhead. In the sanctuary, I saw scores of young men and women flanked by older generations. The entire room was surrounded by memorial flowers. The scent stirred through the chapel as large numbers of people waved cardboard fans. Weak chords came from the organ. Several hundred people filled the church. In front of the pulpit sat a silver open coffin.

A door on the right side of the room opened. Danny's parents, brothers, sisters, and fiancée entered. They walked slowly to the coffin. They hung on each other. Each one stared into the face in the casket. They spoke to Danny, and kissed him. Men and women.

Danny's fiancée moved to face the casket.

No one stirred.

After a minute a brother led her to a seat among the family. Crowds of people from the church queued to pass the coffin.

When the line ended, the organ ceased. The minister rose from behind the pulpit. He shuffled until he stood in full view overlooking the dead waterman. The minister ran his eyes slowly over the faces of Danny's family and smiled. His face twitched slightly.

"Brothers and sisters," he began. "We are gathered here today to honor . . ." The voice faltered. The minister's eyes rolled skyward. He began again with a smile and louder voice: . . ."to honor the memory of Daniel Lednum, who, like too many of the men of this island, has been claimed by the water. We are here to share the tragedy of his family and to help carry the grief of this sweet young woman to whom Daniel would so soon have been wed.

"Death is the enemy we must all face. We must all make our peace with him. All must settle our debits and credits. Far be it for me to say how young Daniel stood with his God. It is a private thing between each sinner and the Almighty. But I can tell you this."

The preacher began to stride back and forth. His voice gained timbre. Pews creaked as people came awake.

"I can tell you that Daniel is so much more happy now than those he has left behind. He sees the power and the glory that we cannot yet imagine. He is at peace beyond the water.

"But why Daniel? Why this tender young man who was bringing so much joy and hope to all of us? Why has the

Lord chosen to take such a youthful spirit from us? Oh, how I have pondered this question. Oh, how, for these many days of grief, have I been praying for God to give me an answer. Why Daniel? Where is the rightness in this death?

"Well, now I know. The rightness is here." The minister spread his arms over the congregation. "The rightness is here in the drawing together of this island community to help support the pain and grief of Daniel's beloved. It is in this pulling together of clammers, crabbers, buyers, oystermen, and their families that we can see the truth in Daniel's death. This can be a lonely, harsh world if we fail to pull together and care for our brothers. But if we live by the golden rule as Jesus has taught us, if we love one another and believe in the peace of the Kingdom of God, where is death's wound? Gone. What need we fear? Nothing. Daniel knows that now, and that is the divine truth he has given us. For who knows when the Lord will call him. And who knows who next will cross the bar?

"Let us pray together the Twenty-third Psalm. The Lord is my shepherd . . ."

Men and women spoke the psalm loudly. Rain beat against the windows and roof.

An undertaker closed the coffin. A line of watermen bore flowers to a waiting seafood truck. Somewhere far back in the procession six young men carried the remains of Danny Lednum out into the rain.

Crabs grew scarce after Danny Lednum's death. The pleasures of the harbor held many watermen ashore. The southwest breeze brought only slight relief from tropical temperatures. As time passed the crowd of basket sitters along the waterfront swelled. Language grew rougher. The old rivalries began to emerge. When I joined the crowd one afternoon looking for Bart Murphy, I was attacked.

"What do you care, boy? I wouldn't tell you where the low-down scum is if I knew. And I know!" A thin bare-chested man with a deep, red sunburn spat at my feet and threw his half-empty beer can into the Narrows. The man spread his legs and began to sway left and right, slowly. His hands squeezed in and out of fists.

"Bart's gettin' some crabs for me."

"Shit, no one's got crabs. But suppose Bart does; why would he want to give 'em to you?"

"Bart's my friend," I said firmly. I smiled. I didn't know the tall man but I wasn't going to act sheepish in front of the basket sitters.

"Neither o' you got friends. That's what I say. And you know what else I say? I say I ain't never liked Bart Murphy, and I don't think I like you." The tall man spit at my feet again and cracked open another beer. The basket sitters smiled at each other.

"Didn't ask you to like me," I said. "Didn't ask you to like Bart. Just tell me where you've seen him and we'll be square."

"Like hell. I don't owe you nothin'. I could tell you where I seen Bart, but I don't like your looks. You look like one o' those St. Michaels Marshalls. Screw you. Screw them. Half Harrison and half Marshall that's what they are. Scum and slime. You're a snake."

The basket sitters raised their eyebrows. I began to lose my patience: "What's family have to do with this? Where's Bart?'

"Don't you change the subject, boy! You're just tryin' to get out o' this. Don't you move or I'll bust you. Gonna settle with you in my own way."

"All right, forget I asked you anything." I started to walk away.

"Hell, you say. Forget nothin'. I told you too many times to stay away from my fishin' holes. Now I'm goin' to teach you not to work my spots."

"I don't know what you are talking about." The basket sitters seemed puzzled, too.

"Liar. You were right on the seaplane wreck when I got my party out there yesterday. You ain't the only sport fisherman, you know."

"Really, I don't know what you're talking about. Let's just forget it." I turned to walk away. The sport fisherman grabbed my arm and spun me around.

"I ain't finished with you. I got claims on them holes. You stay out o' them. Only reason I seen that son-of-a-bitch Bart Murphy workin' down on the flats is cause I had to run way over there to find some fish. You were in my spot."

"So," I said, "Bart Murphy's on the flats. Guess it will take him another hour to get home. I'll come back in a while." I turned to walk away again, glad for the information on Bart, glad to put an end to the confrontation. But the tall fisherman grabbed my arm again. I faced him. His red cheeks began to quiver as he realized he had supplied information he wanted to withhold.

"Damn you, Bob Marshall, put 'em up." The tall man raised his fists.

I stepped back, "Hey, I'm not Bob Marshall."

"Liar. Not Bob Marshall, chickenshit!"

"Bob Marshall? That boy ain't Bob Marshall," said one of the basket sitters. "You pickin' on him because you think he's Marshall? Better sober up and look again."

"Not Bob Marshall?" asked the fisherman, still not comprehending. "Not Bob Marshall?" The fisherman squinted hard at me.

"Not Bob Marshall," I repeated.

The fisherman's fists loosened slightly. "Really?"

"Really, I've never been a fishing boat captain in my life." I told him my name.

"Boy's right," said a number of onlookers.

The fisherman kept repeating my name. His feet pawed the ground; his eyes watched them. "Then I guess fightin's off," he said. "Yeah, I guess fightin's off 'til I find that scum Marshall. Damn, boy, your looks ain't doin' you any favors."

The fisherman disappeared down a road of oyster shells. The scuffing of his feet could be heard a long time after he was out of sight. The basket sitters laughed.

"Christ that was comic."

"He's on a rampage."

"Guess you better stand clear o' him 'til he sobers up."

I nodded.

"Jackie'll never remember. Goin' to go after you again, boy. Next time he sees you. Guess if I was drunk I might think you was Bob Marshall, too."

"Wonder if Bob know's that old drunk's on a jag."

"Doubt it."

"Best tell him: something crazy could happen."

"Let Randy tell him. Randy ought to meet the man whose hide he almost fought for."

I agreed.

In the row of slips where fishing party boats tie up, I searched for my look-a-like. I walked along the lines of old white crab boats that had been converted for carrying fishing parties, but all of the men I saw were well past middle age. I asked about Marshall's location.

Several old men looked up from cleaning fish, scowled, and pointed down the wharf. "At the sign," they said.

"Long blue thing, called *Finn Tann* or something like that. Looks like a yacht."

"Ain't never seen a blue fishin' boat before, have you?"

"It's bad luck's what it is."

"Not for Bobby."

"For us."

"Boy's got queer ways. Sure ain't no Tilghman Islander."

"Right good waterman, anyhow."

"But different."

"Youngest man ever got his Coast Guard license in Bal'mer. Loaded with fish when some come home 'bout empty."

"He got a mess a parties that come regular. Some of 'ems just meat hunters."

"Well, Bobby's the man for 'em."

"He's one fishin' fool for sure."

I found the sign—"Robert Marshall: fishing parties"—and the blue boat.

"I like it," I said out loud.

"Then you must be a tourist or a Jonah," drawled a young voice from somewhere in Marshall's boat.

"No more than your damn boat," I said. It was an involuntary response.

"Guess you aren't a tourist." Bob Marshall rose out of the cockpit—sturdy, medium build, tan, face like cupid, frazzled, sun-bleached hair.

We stared at each other: we both wore blue-jean cut-offs, T-shirts, and boat moccasins.

A smile of recognition broke over Marshall's face. He spoke, "Then what are you, my long-lost twin brother?"

"Some people think its closer than that."

"Then I guess they want to fight you."

"That's about what it comes to."

"And you've come to see the root of your troubles."

"Something like that," I said.

"Then you'll drink a beer."

"If I can buy."

"No. That's taken care of." Marshall opened a cooler

packed with ice and Budweiser. "But you can help me scrub down the boat."

I had already spotted an unused mop.

As we scrubbed the blue boat I introduced myself and gave a quick sketch of how I had come from Pennsylvania. I told about my near fight with the tall fisherman and warned Marshall that the man was out for him.

Marshall chuckled. He explained why he had some enemies on the island: "First of all I've worked for the best of these party-boat captains. I was a mate for years. Sometimes I didn't even get paid; just went with these captains for the experience. I learned a lot from them. One guy taught me about bluefish, another about rock, another about trout, another about dealing with people. I respect these fishermen, but some of them can't get it into their heads that I'm grown up. I was "the boy" on party boats for so long it's hard for a lot of people around here to think of me as a captain. But I've had my own boat for eight years now.

"Still, some of these guys don't want to give me the same rights on the water that any party captain should have. Looks like that's what caused you trouble. Your friend's a good fisherman, but he's had some bad days lately. We all have. There are a couple of little holes out here where I know I can always find fish. No one's got a claim on them. If I get to a hole first, then it's my spot for the day. That's the custom around here, but some of these guys can't cope with "the boy" beating them to a good hole. It's too bad they feel that way, but I'm not backin' down. It's my Bay, too. Guess I bring some of this on myself."

"With this blue yacht and all," I said. "This just isn't the Tilghman style."

"I guess that's part of it, but these old watermen have kind of gotten used to my blue boat. They figure it'll Jonah me. They're safe as long as they don't come aboard.

"See, I'm not a born Tilghman Islander. That can cause you troubles. Maybe it's more trouble for me than you, 'cause I'm half from Tilghman. M'Ada Harrison's my grandmother, but my mother ran up the road to marry a St. Michaels waterman, Junior Marshall. You can guess how happy that made all the Harrisons on Tilghman, and . . ."

I broke into a laugh: I was beginning to see the similarities between Bobby and his father.

By the time we had scrubbed the last traces of blood and scales from *Finn Tann*, I had a new job. I would start as Bob Marshall's mate the next morning. There was only one problem: I knew nothing about fin-fishing.

The fishing party was from Wilmington, Delaware, and they planned to arrive at *Finn Tann* at the civilized hour of 8:30. Bob Marshall and I met on the boat at 7:30 to prepare the fishing gear. Marshall started a pot of coffee brewing on an alcohol stove and spread red, yellow, and green coils of surgical tubing over one of the two engine boxes. To this collection, Marshall added a box of hooks, loops of stainless steel wire, and a handful of swivels used to connect the business end of fishing tackle to the line.

"Make up some new lures," said Marshall serving coffee.

I thought it was a command. I didn't want to betray my inexperience, so I mimicked Marshall as I picked up hook, wire, and swivel. Using a pair of pliers Bob Marshall cut a twelve-inch span of wire, twisted it through the eyes of hook and swivel, and threaded the metal backbone through a pre-cut piece of red tubing. A commercial-looking bluefish lure was the result—it looked like an eel. Marshall twisted a spiral into the body of the lure so it would spin in the water and give the appearance of swimming.

The construction of the lure took Marshall only a minute or two. The concept seemed simple enough, but my mimicry began to fail me when I couldn't thread the hook, wire, and swivel through the surgical tubing. The wire jammed and twisted.

"Nice try," said Marshall. His eyes sparkled with amusement. "Don't believe I got as far as you have when I started to make my first lure. Let me show you: it takes a little time to learn this. First, you have to lubricate the wire. Spit on it . . ."

I didn't have to fake experience any longer. Marshall didn't seem impatient or disturbed that I was a green crewman.

"O.K. Help me," I said. "I'm lost."

"Well, I hope so. If you caught onto this on the first try, then you'd be the captain and I'd be the mate before the day was over. Look here: first . . ." Marshall led me slowly through the process of making lures.

After two clumsy efforts and encouragement from Marshall, I constructed a lure that Marshall said "would work." I repeated the process several times to anchor the skills in my mind. Slowly my speed increased. To my unprofessional eye my lures began to look more like those made by the captain. Marshall watched silently. Only once the fisherman intervened: he grabbed my hands securely as I held a lure and pondered how to put the spiral in the body. Marshall snapped my wrists in opposite directions. The eel twisted into a neat spiral.

"That's all there is to it. Ready for lesson number two?"

By the time a new Ford pulled into the parking space in front of *Finn Tann*'s slip on the Narrows, I had learned three different knots for tying lures to lines, how to rig sinkers on trawling lines, and how to regulate the weight of sinkers according to a fisherman's station on the boat.

Four men in their sixties emerged from the car. They wore baseball caps and khaki vests stitched with pockets for all kinds of fishing equipment. Two of the men carried rod-holders on their belts.

"You didn't need to get so dressed up for us, Bobby," called a raspy voice from the Ford group.

"Don't tease the captain, Charlie," said another voice. "He might not have any better clothes. You know about these poor watermen, don't you?"

"That's the first true thing I've ever heard you say, Sammy," said Marshall. "With the little money you guys pay me, you're lucky I'm not out here bare ass."

"Just about looks like you might be with all those patches on your shorts," said a man handing a beer cooler onto *Finn Tann*.

"Don't take it personally, Jack. I give everyone the same royal treatment," said the fisherman.

"Now *that* I can believe."

"You better, if you want to catch some fish."

"Aye, aye, captain," chorused the men who had chartered *Finn Tann*.

Marshall introduced me—"another hippie fisherman you'll have to put up with." We shook hands all around. Marshall started the engines. I cast off lines. The first round of Bloody Marys spread among the party. *Finn Tann* headed for Poplar Island flats.

I steered the boat. Bob Marshall arranged rods, watched the flashing lights on the depth sounder for signs of fish, and bantered with his party.

"What do you have for us today, Captain Robert?"

"I think we might find you a few blues—if you're nice."

"Blues! What happened to all the rockfish?"

"You boys got greedy last time; caught 'em all. You won't see another rock 'til next spring."

"He's right, Sammy. We caught so many of those thirty-pounders my arms were sore for a week."

"I know I'm right. You boys have got to learn to take it

easy. I don't want one of these fish givin' you a heart attack out here."

"You're a conniving one, Bobby. I know you just want to save your special rockfish holes for some other parties. You don't like us."

"Well, if you guys would come up with a tip once in a while . . ."

"All right we get the message, but I'm just teasing you, Bob." The tallest of the party clapped his arm around Marshall's shoulder and gave the captain a rough hug. "Bluefish are fine; just put us on to them. Let's have another drink of breakfast." The party drank two more rounds of Bloody Marys.

Marshall directed my course and paced around the fishing deck of the boat. He scanned the water. He watched the movement of gulls. Isolated birds glided here and there. Some small flocks flapped together close to the surface. Suddenly a flock of birds wheeled fifteen to twenty feet off the water. The Bay beneath churned as hundreds of silver alewives, bait fish, broke into the sunlight.

"There," called Marshall even before the bait fish broke the surface. "Pour it to her. Get your rods. Sammy stand aft, Jack, take the starboard waist; Charlie . . ." The captain positioned the fishing party. A steep wake tumbled from *Finn Tann* as I accelerated the boat in the direction of the wheeling gulls.

"Let out your lines men. Let the sinkers bump the bottom three times. A little more line, Charlie; that's good, Jack; OK Sammy, you got one; you too, Harry. Drinkin's over gentlemen; let's fish."

All four lines on the boat were taut. The men sawed back and forth with their rods, working the bluefish. The lines pulled left and right abruptly as the fish fought the fishermen. The men began to pant and swear at their opponents.

"Come on you blue son-of-a-bitch."

"Bring it home, you mother."

"Fight me, bastard."

"Give me help, boy!"

I knew the command was aimed at me. The smallest of the men, a dark Sicilian named Sammy, had reeled in his line until only the fifteen-foot monofilament leader strung between the rod and a two-foot-long bluefish, leaping from the water at the stern of the boat.

I was supposed to grab the leader and pull the fish aboard with a hand-over-motion. I began quickly. The monofilament cut my hand as the fish strained to break loose. When I had the fish within three feet of my grasp, I doubled the leader over my right hand and heaved the three-pound blue aboard.

"Gaff him into the bait box," said Marshall.

I grabbed the short-handled gaff and caught the bluefish by the gill. Next I began pulling the fish one way and the hook and line the other. I thought this was the way I had seen it done in films. The hook pulled out of the fish with the sound of ripping cartilage. The wounded fish vomited blood and alewives all over the deck.

"Jesus," said one of the party wrinkling his face. "We've got a puker . . . and this boy's a butcher."

"Calm down, Charlie; there's some that gaff fish that way. Randy just doesn't know the clean way to do it," said Marshall, leaving the wheel and landing a fish for one of the men.

"Gaff blues like this," Marshall handed a fish line and the gaff to me. "Catch the gaff under the hook, pull the line straight down, twist your wrist to unset the hook, and snap: the hook pops clean out and the fish falls in the ice box."

I slowly repeated the process with the next fish I landed. Marshall talked me through the steps. Snap. The fish fell free. No blood, no vomit.

Two voices called, "Little help, boys!" I had more fish to land.

My hands burned from the strain of the cutting leaders. After I gaffed every fish into an ice box set in the middle of the fishing deck, Bob Marshall and I hurried to wrench the eel lures back into their spiral profile and drop the lines overboard again. The calls—"let's go, let's go, boys"—from the party kept us in motion. The men in the party wanted no break from fighting blues, but they wanted the vessel clear of loose, snapping fish and tangled lines. Fish reeled alongside two and three per minute. I kept up with the landings.

Marshall watched to make sure each man in the party was catching his share of fish. The captain changed lures and sinker weights frequently. The adjustments increased the pace of landings. Everyone caught fish. After forty-five minutes of riding south with the school of bluefish, the party seemed relieved when Marshall let *Finn Tann* slip away from the school. Sweat ran freely. Marshall pulled off his shirt. I followed the example. The men in the fishing party dove for the beer cooler. They drank Heineken as if it were lemonade.

"Sixty-five fish," said Marshall, wiping the sweat from his forehead with a towel. "Here, you need it." He tossed the towel to me.

"I'd call that some fair fishing, Robert," said one of the party. "But there weren't any ten or twelve pounders in the batch."

I could still feel blood throbbing through my arms.

Marshall could see I was excited. "You ain't seen nothin' yet," he said. "If these gentlemen can get their wind back, I guess we have to find 'em some bigger fish . . . now that they're warmed up and all."

"You think we aren't ready?" bantered the small Sicilian.

"I'd never say that about you, Sammy. Anyone can tell you're a hunter," Marshall smiled.

"Just you find us those big ones, boy."

"OK, don't put your rods away. Careful with the beer. Heart attack fishing comin' up."

The fishing party lounged around a table in the cabin. They swilled several beers apiece and made cold-cut submarine sandwiches from packages of meats, cheeses, and condiments spread in front of them. I heard slips of their conversation:

"Magnificent fishing."

"A good day if we went home now."

"None of these other boats were on the fish like we were."

"Robert's a great captain—always on the lookout."

"Couple of those devils 'bout tore my shoulders out—didn't want to die."

"This is the life."

"Yeah, but I could go for a fight with a few monsters."

"After a nap."

"Yeah, after a nap."

For the next hour most of the party slept. Occasionally one of the men set out his line. Marshall obliged him by finding a small school and trailing along the edge of it. The man would hook fish regularly, but not enough to disturb the sleepers or make me sweat.

The captain talked quietly to me: "That's the trouble with days like this; we should go home now. Got a couple hundred pounds of fish, but people don't think they got their money's worth unless they're out on the water 'til four. Got to do a lot of driftin' around like this—to waste time. Later on I'll put 'em on a big school that'll tire 'em out. Then everyone will want to go home."

The party revived with the making of more sandwiches and the popping of beers; Bob Marshall began searching the horizon for signs of "the big school."

North of Poplar Island several flocks of gulls careened close to the surface of the Bay. The engines on *Finn Tann* kicked into a deep roar. All of the other sport fishermen in the area continued to drift, but Marshall charged his boat into Eastern Bay. Dead ahead, the flocks of gulls began spiraling high in the air. Acres of bluefish broke the surface all around *Finn Tann*.

"Goddamn, look at these monsters, Charlie."

"Bobby's put us on 'em now."

"Got 'em all to ourselves; those other boats are just beginning to notice what we're into."

"Strike! My God, I've got a whale."

"Strike here, too. Like to carry away my gear."

Marshall caught my eye and winked.

"Little help, boy."

"Gaff here, boy."

"Lure's carried away: quick another!"

I ran around the boat trying to keep up with the needs of the party. The water foamed with ten-pound bluefish. The fish struck the lures as soon as they hit the water. My ears began to ring with the call of "strike," and my hands grew numb from fighting fish and leaders aboard. After landing thirty fish in less than ten minutes, I found an old pair of garden gloves for relief from the bite of the monofilament.

"Hurry, boy!"

"Get my line out!"

"What a battle!"

"Don't slow me down."

"Throw them on the floor."

"Come on, suckers."

The party was so eager to catch more fish they were content with Marshall and me gaffing blues onto the floor of *Finn Tann*, instead of taking the time to gaff the fish into the ice chest. In spare seconds Marshall and I scooped snapping blues away from the men's legs. The main ice chest and a hundred-pound spare overflowed. Fish leaped, flashed teeth, and splattered blood over the decks.

"Get the garbage cans," called Marshall.

I emptied trash onto the cabin floor from the two fifty-gallon plastic barrels and hauled them out on deck. Marshall began pitching fish into the barrels.

"Strike."

"Strike, again."

"Boy! Help me fight him!"

Bob and I both grabbed the rod from a man in the stern whose legs were buckling. As we gripped the rod, the man staggered forward into the cabin. He crumpled onto a bench seat and wheezed loudly. We reeled aboard the fish and turned to watch the exhausted party. Marshall caught my gaze and rolled his eyes in a way that said, "God, this is enough."

"O.K. Reel 'em in, gentlemen," said Marshall.

"Not yet; I haven't got my fifteen pounder!"

"There it is, Charlie. It just took your bait. Come on, bring 'em aboard. Save some for the poor people."

The party gave in. I landed the last fish. Charlie had his fifteen pounder. The trash buckets were full. Crew and party sat down on the engine boxes and drank a round of beers. It took that long for us to catch our breath. The boat drifted in the current. The wheezer recovered from exhaustion. We had more than 500 pounds of meat aboard—140 bluefish. The party congratulated each other.

Marshall slapped me on the back, "Tired?"

"Maybe."

"Hell of a life isn't it?"

"It's not farming or teaching school."

"Yeah, it's a bloody battle."

"I kind of like it."

"It's the fight," said Bob. "Yeah, if it were up to me I'd just catch fish for the sport. Throw 'em back when the fight's over."

In late summer the corn stalks stretched brown above the Miles River, and the crabs came so steadily that the price per bushel fell below eight dollars. The watermen's skiffs stayed tied to their moorings, and the Carpenter Street Tavern filled with men by noon. I drifted in after fishing and listened to the jabber:

"No sense working 'til the price o' jimmies comes higher, know it *will*, too!"

"Yeah, I guess it's time t' help them boys git their log canoes ready for the race."

The men talked on: not about work, but about log canoes —the watermen's rodeo.

"Junie Marshall sure got one heavy old boat, don't he?"

" 'Deed he do, but he'll keep her charging like a Tilghman boy in a brawl. Might surprise them Chestertown boats."

"I don't believe it; gonna be Jimmy Wilson they got to beat. Hear he been to the sailmaker again with his mainsail. Gettin' it right, ya know."

"I want to tell you something," said Bart Murphy. "I ain't goin' to say Junie'll win many races, but damn if he don't upset his canoe more 'n common."

"I'll go along with that," said Billy Adams. "You remember Fourth of July when Junior . . ."

"Oh, Christ, Billy's tellin' stories on me again." Junior Marshall stood in the entrance to the bar with a tool kit in his left hand and a coil of heavy wire over his right shoulder. "What in God's name have I done to be the topic of conversation with such a prominent group of citizens?"

"You mean a bunch o' derelicts," shouted a woman from the end of the bar.

"That's what I'm sayin', Miss Slim," said Junior. "Looks like the whole goddamn bunch o' them are just what I need to race *Rover* this weekend."

"What's a matter, Junie; lose your crew again?"

"Ain't that, Pete. I'm just givin' the boys a little vacation."

"I'm sure they're complainin' real loud, too. After you upset over to Oxford last week."

"They'll get over it, but I might be lookin' for some new blood." Junior slipped up to Bart and threw a full-nelson on the waterman and gave a belly laugh.

Murphy broke the wrestling hold, "Give Junie a Black Label 'fore he hurts hisself, Jake."

"Tend jib, Bart."

"Damn if I can't."

"Just this weekend."

"I have to work."

"Hell with it."

"Junie, what do I want to give up a day o' crabbin' for: just to go upset your goddamn log canoe?"

"Leave Bart be, Junie: he's an old dog. Too old to mess with sailboats. Ask him if this past year weren't the last winter for the *Ruby Ford*," said the bartender. "Bart's goin' into eeling full time with Big Henry."

Bart got to his feet and gave the bartender a dirty look: "Sissy baby talk. I'm sailin', Junie. And Randy looks just right to ride onto the outrigger."

"That's just how I figure it," said Junior.

The Labor Day Regatta began on Friday. All day long canoe sailors and yachts gravitated toward the Miles River Yacht Club. Many of the racing canoes were from St. Michaels and one-by-one they lined up along the Yacht Club shore. A sixty-foot power yacht had arrived in town towing two canoes and twenty-five sailors from Chestertown, forty miles up the Bay. The parking lot filled with pitched tents, campers, and vans. At first, canoe crews drifted around the club in definable groups: red shirts here, green shirts there, no shirts heading for the pool.

Bart and I were part of the crew for Junior's *Rover*, and we walked along docks where canoes were tied. We looked over the competition.

Junior explained to me that log canoes are descendants of Indian dugouts. Racing canoes are made of five logs fastened together and hollowed out. Before gasoline engines and planked skiffs, log canoes were the boats oystermen tonged from, but since the twenties watermen have used their sailing canoes only for racing. They are 25–35 feet long, 5½–8½ feet abeam, and capable of carrying as much as 2,000 square feet of sail on two masts as tall as 60 feet.

Some canoes had blue or yellow hulls with yacht finishes, while others looked as though they'd received the workboat-white housepaint treatment for the eightieth time. In one canoe the go-fast gear consisted of a beer cooler and a five-gallon bailing bucket; another boat sported some aluminum spars, new sails, and stays on the foremast.

Junior Marshall tossed a jest at the crew of a colorful canoe, "Seems like putting yellow sails on a log canoe is like taking a whore to Sunday School, don't it, though?"

Someone replied: "You still catching oysters with that old boat of yours? Those shells in the bilges must slow her down."

Everyone within earshot began to chuckle. Within minutes the red alligator shirts had mixed with the Budweiser hats to joke about the pros and cons of a canoe mast made from a Nixon-era National Christmas Tree. A woman canoe sailor challenged a waterman to an arm-wrestling contest. In the clubhouse men from different crews clustered together and retold the rumor they'd heard alleging that the world-famous sailor and sailmaker Ted Hood might be coming to sail a log canoe for which he had just cut new sails. Ted Turner, Hoods's chief adversary, was coming to sail another canoe because Hood was racing. The story was apocryphal: Hood and Turner were off in England at the Admiral's Cup Race.

At 10:00 on Saturday morning, Bart, Junior Marshall, and I joined other canoe sailors working at a uniform task—rigging the boats for the 11:30 race. The morning was hot, and the strain of hoisting two fifty-foot masts into place filled my eye-sockets with sweat. Junior peeled to his bare chest. Bart lingered over icing down the cooler of soda and beer. Silently we unbagged sails, attached sprits and clubs, and sorted the maze of lines into meaningful order.

We did all of this with unsolicited comments from a group that hovered close to *Rover*. Bobbie Marshall, Ginny Adams, Dougie Spurry, and others were full of advice:

"Don't you think you better cleat that horse rope more securely?"

"Don't fall off that outrigger, Randy. You might get run over."

"You done any swimmin' practice, Bart?"

"Give your wallet here—just in case."

"Well, I guess you're ready, Junior's got his eyeglasses strapped on."

"Cheers."

As *Rover* pushed out from shore and we began raising our sails I noticed that every canoe had a following of wives, husbands, friends, and wharf rats. I heard canoe sailors call them "tenders." Many of these tenders rode in powerboats that provided support for the canoes. The tenders towed some of the canoes through shoal water and the crowded anchorage. Tenders patrolled just to the lee of the race course to help save a cooler or unstep a mast if "their" canoe capsized. Several boatloads of tenders flashed hand-held red speed-limit signs to warn passing pleasure craft to proceed with caution in the vicinity of the log canoe race.

At 11:20 the canoes timed their starting tacks in a seven-knot breeze. I rode on *Rover*'s outrigger, a frame extension six feet beyond the stern of the boat. From there my weight acted to counterbalance the weight of the canoe's bowsprit and jib. I held a line that trimmed the canoe's mainsail. Bart crouched in the bow of *Rover* and handled the line that trimmed the boat's jib. Two men I did not know rode on *Rover*'s springboards. These were planks that stretched across the beam of the boat and reached ten feet to windward. The men climbed in and out on the springboards, adjusting their position so that their weight counteracted the wind's efforts to capsize the canoe. Junior Marshall steered with both hands on the long, varnished tiller and examined a race course chart on his lap. The wake of the boat hissed six inches beneath the seat of my pants.

On the course the canoes moved fast under their great goose-wing sails. The spectator fleet (crabbing boats, cruisers, and every other kind of hull with an engine) and tenders waited at the lee end of the line—the grandstands. People poured their first beverages, the sun flared, and the fans jumped into the role of "backseat skipper." *Mystery*, the tallest-rigged canoe, sliced by the fans on a reach. From several tenders came remarks:

"Looka there!"

"Ain't she purty."

"Neither another boat like that one."

"Lordy, she's a sailboat."

"Yessir, she's right."

Rover's crew hardly noticed the sound of the five-minute gun; we were embroiled in speculation about *Mystery*.

"That's some light air boat," said Bart.

"Damn if old cap'n Bill can't sail her, too," said Junior.

"That's the smart of her sure."

"Jimmy Wilson goin' to get a fight today."

"This ain't his kind o' air."

"Ain't *Rover*'s either," said Junior. "But long as Bart's quick to free that jib we aren't like to upset."

"Jus' don't you worry, Junie. I'm sensitive about gettin' wet," said Bart. "But would you look there at Jimmy!"

A large white canoe with black bottom paint overtook us to windward. She carried a crew of ten. The shirtless man at the helm chainsmoked as he steered. His black chest hair was slick with sweat.

"Don't you know that boy's got to win," said Junie Marshall.

"Owes it to his family."

"That's what I heard, too. His daddy courted his mother in that canoe."

"*Magic*'s some special boat, for sure. They say she's cost Jimmy more than . . . ."

Gun.

"Trim her up," shouted Junior. "Good, Bart. Ease her a bit, Randy. Come in some, boys."

Spray from *Rover*'s wake made a fine rooster tail and fell on my hot legs. We sprinted for the starting line.

Fans jumped to their feet.

"Go, Captain Bill."

"Come on Jimmy, get out of that pack."

"Hound 'em, Junior."

"That blue boat's barging."

"Hey, you're barging."

"They're gonna hit."

"Damn, they're liable to kill someone."

"Watch that bowsprit!"

"Free the sheets," yelled Marshall.

"Who spilled my beer . . ."

A bowsprit crashed across my legs and pinned me against the back rest of the outrigger. Four canoes piled up around *Rover* at the buoy marking the windward end of the line. Sails fluttered limply overhead. It looked as though one of the smaller boats had barged into *Mystery* and set off a chain of collisions. *Mystery*'s skipper patiently asked the alleged offender if she (the only woman skipper) wanted to change course as crews fended off. Another crewman and I forced *Rover* free from our tangle with the bowsprit. *Mystery* stepped ahead of the fleet. *Rover* ghosted behind.

We stayed there. The wind blew gently and *Mystery* went about her business of making up the time she owed other boats. Going around the first mark she spread her kite (a sunfish sail) on the top of the foremast and hung a squaresail from the top of her main. Jimmy Wilson followed suit, so did we. *Rover* was third.

Things got festive. Billy Adams, who tended *Rover* in his *Yankie*, joined up late. He was alone.

"Hey, Billy, you 'bout missed the race. Where you been at?" called Junior.

"Price o' crabs went to twelve dollars this mornin'."

"Shit," mumbled Bart.

"It was good crabbin' this mornin', is what it was," continued Billy.

"Don't tell me about it," said Bart.

"Made me more 'n spare change. Every time I dipped a crab I thought about poor Bart missin' one right fine . . ."

"Would you listen to this," began Bart. "I'm goin' to tell you what it is. Ain't either St. Michaels waterman goin' to bring home more 'n one bushel 'o crabs for every five a Tilghman boy catches."

"If he's catchin'," said Billy, "and ain't floatin' around in a sailboat or pourin' profits into the Carpenter Street."

"Damn if it isn't the pot callin' the kettle black," said Junior. "Sail the boat. We're losin' ground."

Rover had slipped back into the middle of the fleet during the long, slow, downwind leg of the race. Bart adjusted the jib slightly and pulled two beers from the ice chest. He threw one across fifteen feet of water to Billy and sighed, "Looks like a two-case race."

"Yep, an over-the-side day," admitted Junior.

"How about a crab sandwich?" asked Billy.

"Nothing better going on," said Bart. "Give up crabbin' any time for excitement like this." He yawned sarcastically.

Then *Rover* caught a puff near shore. The crew dropped their beers into the bilge and scrambled out on the springboards. Water poured over the lee gunwale. A crewman bailed buckets full of water overboard. I felt the outrigger sink into the waves.

A chorus sounded across the water, "There she goes, she's going."

To windward of *Rover* a canoe floundered with her lee gunwale awash. She shipped water with all of her crew perched on the springboards. The canoe teetered. The man on the outrigger fell overboard. The boat rolled over, and crew began swimming around retrieving loose gear. Two tenders went to the rescue. Fans cheered.

Rover steadied herself and moved on.

"Too many girls on that boat," said Bart.

"Got struck by a tornado up the creek," added Junior. "Must a been our jib tender saved us."

"Bart ain't no sissy baby," said Billy.

The race turned out to be a duel between Wilson's *Magic* and *Mystery*. A slight wind picked up after the leaders rounded the final buoy, and they put another quarter mile between them and the rest of the canoes.

Rover held her place in the middle of the fleet. In the boat no one talked. We hoped that *Rover* would not lose the puff she was riding along the shoreline. Bart hunkered down forward in the bilge. Two men leaned part way out on the hiking boards. Junior steered. I braced against the back rest of the outrigger. For a change, no one moved. Any shift in weight might disturb *Rover*'s progress.

We sailed four miles that way before shoal water forced *Rover* to come about, and we lost most of the wind.

"Goddamn it," said Junior. "Pass me the bucket. I been holdin' my bladder a right good while. We ain't sailin'. May as well take care o' business—take a load off me and this canoe."

Yankie came alongside after making a quick trip into St. Michaels Harbor. The boat carried ten girls in bikinis. We counted them. Billy Adams stood barechested at the wheel and smiled to himself. He was the only man aboard.

Then Billy cast a glance at the crew of *Rover* out of the corner of his eye, "Ain't my social life improvin', boys?"

The girls twittered.

Ginny Adams emerged from *Yankie*'s cabin. She heard Billy's remark. Ginny put her hands on her hips and spoke so everyone on both boats could hear her: "Improvin' to a point, Mr. Adams. Improvin' to a *certain* point. Billy's lookin', but the bottom'll fall out o' this boat 'fore he's touchin'. Trust me!"

A cannon sounded. Far ahead *Mystery*, then *Magic*, crossed the finish line. On shore *Mystery*'s tenders tapped a celebration beer keg. Forty-five minutes later we sailed in front of the committee boat at the end of the race. Junior ordered us to drop the sails and we took a tow from *Yankie*.

Canoe sailors clustered around the beer keg on the Yacht Club lawn. As we tied *Rover* along the dock men began throwing jibes at Marshall about our slow finish:

"Hey, Junie, you and your boys should have stayed out on

the water. Make sure you're ready for tomorrow's race."

"Believe we'd done just that 'fore we come ashore with you, but . . . we're out o' beer."

"It's that Tilghman Island bunch slowed you down, Junie. Not one of them seen a sailboat before," shouted a tall man.

The next thing the tall man knew Bart was dragging him across the lawn toward the harbor. Other men joined the struggle. People threw beer. Bart and the tall man toppled off a bulkhead into the water.

They came out laughing. The men knew each other well. The tall man was a pleasure boat sailor. Bart sailed workboats. Reasons enough for roughhousing.

The party lasted late into the night. Few people talked seriously about tomorrow's race. Everyone seemed to assume that Jimmy Wilson would win—"Boy wants it bad." His winning would mark the end of the summer log canoe racing season.

The end of summer seemed to play in the back of everyone's mind. Junior Marshall spent more than an hour talking to boatbuilder Sam McQuay about hauling *Rover* out of the water and replacing more of her bottom. Billy and Ginny Adams sat at the bar and wondered aloud to each other whether Ginny should quit her job at the ribbon factory to go early tonging with Billy when the season opened in two weeks. Bart Murphy and a seafood buyer speculated on the price of oysters during the coming season. Then Bart turned to me. He said that in a few days he was going to gather together Charlie Buck, Bernard, Bobby, and the rest of a dredging crew to patch and paint *Ruby Ford* for another season of oystering. The skipjack race would be coming soon.

I would not be making that race. I would return to teaching because I love it the way Bart Murphy loves standing at the wheel of the *Ruby Ford*. But I was turning back ashore with gratitude for the time I had spent on the water. I had followed the watermen through the seasons of oysters, eels, crabs, and fin fish. During those seasons the idealized images of the watermen's lives, which I had built from *Captains Courageous* and *Moby Dick*, had dissolved. Yet my romance with the waterman's life remained. Now romance rooted in the people I knew and the hours they had shared with me. I had not found specific traces of my colonial ancestors on Bay Hundred. That did not matter. I had found friends and a heritage.

Something of that heritage echoed in the words of a song that erupted after midnight from a congregation of watermen gathered around a log canoe on the beach. Snatches of the lyrics rode on the breeze: "Goin' to run all night, goin' to run all day; well, I bet my money on the bobtail nag, somebody bet on the bay."